THE SOUTHERN
THEN & NOW

Half Title: **EAST CROYDON**

Then : 25 May 1963

London Midland Region engines were regular visitors to the Brighton main line, but it was unusual to be able to photograph two at once. A double chimney Class 5, No 44766 on an excursion to the south coast, is taking water before continuing its journey. In the foreground Stanier two-cylinder 2-6-4T No 42430 has just arrived with a parcels train from Willesden Junction.

Now : 29 February 1996

There have been modifications to the track layout and little remains of the old station, which has been extensively reconstructed in the intervening years. However the buildings under the walkway and immediately in front of the Class 73, are probably part of the old station. *Brian Haresnape/Author*

Title Page: **WATERLOO**

Then : 26 August 1966

Unlike the older picture of Waterloo on the cover of this book, this classic view shows the full extent of the station. The picture was taken during the evening peak period – in the foreground, Standard 2-6-4T No 80012 is arriving with empty stock from Clapham Junction, whilst rebuilt 'Battle of Britain' Pacific No 34052 is pulling out with the 6pm train to Salisbury. In the station platforms a variety of trains can be seen including a 4-COR electric unit, 'Warship' and 'Crompton' diesel locomotives, and a Standard Class 5 4-6-0 on the 6.9pm train to Basingstoke. The Windsor line platforms, behind the signalbox on the left of the picture, are clearly identifiable by the lower roof line. They were destined to be the location for the new Waterloo International station as shown in the next picture, which is repeated from the cover for comparison purposes.

Now : 1 February 1995

In order to accommodate the lengthy Eurostar trains, the International station extends well out from main line station. The old signalbox has been demolished and new bridging inserted to accomodate the new tracks. *Brian Stephenson/Brian Morrison*

Front cover, top: **WATERLOO**

Then : 11 June 1985

A general view of the station from the flats on the west side of the line, showing a train leaving for Bournemouth. The roof of the Windsor line platforms can just be seen above the signalbox on the left hand side.

Now : 1 February 1995

For details see title page 'Now' caption above. *Both Brian Morrison*

Front cover, bottom: **PEASMARSH JUNCTION**

Then : 1957

Trains from Guildford to Cranleigh and Horsham branched off the main Portsmouth line at the junction. 'M7' 0-4-4T No 30052 has just passed Peasmarsh Junction signalbox with a train for Horsham. A semi-fast train from Portsmouth to Waterloo is passing on the up line.

Now : 8 November 1995

There is now no trace of the branch at the junction, and even the railway cottages have gone. A Wessex electric is heading south with a train for Portsmouth Harbour. *Both Author*

Back cover, top: **GUILDFORD**

Then : 1962

This view from the road bridge at the south end of the station, shows an Ivatt 2-6-2T leaving with a train for Horsham, composed of a three coach Bulleid set. Part of the coaling stage for the shed can be seen on the left.

Now : 8 November 1995

A section of the area formerly occupied by the shed yard, is now a car park. The branch to Cranleigh and Horsham closed in June 1965. A train for Redhill is leaving the platform once used by Horsham trains. *Both Author*

Back cover, bottom: **WIMBLEDON**

Then : 1959

The bridges which span the line to the west of Wimbledon station, provide an excellent viewpoint to watch the passing trains. 'King Arthur' 4-6-0 No 30802 *Sir Durnore* is heading a relief train to Bournemouth, which is mainly composed of Maunsell stock. This was a typical Summer Saturday holiday express of the 1950s.

Now : 6 November 1995

Present day trains to Southampton and Bournemouth are less visually appealing, if faster and more efficient. This Wessex electric will be down at Southampton in about 1 hour 10 minutes, with two stops. Assuming *Sir Durnore's* journey was non-stop, it is likely to have taken some 20 minutes longer. *Both Author*

THE SOUTHERN
THEN & NOW

MIKE ESAU

Publishing

First published 1996

ISBN 0 7110 2464 2

© Mike Esau 1996

Designed by Jon Stickley & Robert Antell

Published by Ian Allan Publishing

an imprint of Ian Allan Ltd, Terminal House, Station Approach, Shepperton, Surrey TW17 8AS.

Printed by Ian Allan Printing Ltd, Coombelands House, Coombelands Lane, Addlestone, Weybridge, Surrey KT15 1HY.

List of Locations

Please note that, unless stated otherwise, the numbers refer to the photographic sequence and not to page numbers

Introduction

The Southern Then and Now is the third book in Ian Allan's series, covering the territory served by the Southern Railway, later British Railways' Southern Region. The pictures have been divided into the Eastern Section, Central Section and Western Section of the Southern Railway. These Sections broadly equated with the geographical areas served by the South Eastern & Chatham Railway (SECR), the London Brighton & South Coast Railway (LBSCR) and the London & South Western Railway (LSWR) respectively.

With a few exceptions, all the 'Then' pictures were taken during the 20 years or so following Nationalisation in 1948. This was a period of great change, for the closures implemented after the 1963 report — The Reshaping of British Railways — not only drastically reduced track mileage, but also had a knock-on effect on myriad supporting activities. Fortunately, apart from the decimation of routes west of Exeter, the Southern did not fare too badly from the line closures. On the motive power front, the Bournemouth electrification scheme saw the end of steam traction on the Southern Region in 1967.

Travelling round the system, I have been surprised how little some locations have changed, especially those in the London suburban area. As some of the pictures in this book show, other places have altered beyond all recognition, especially where the train service has been withdrawn.

Because of the restricted time allowed for the preparation of the book, I was only able to travel to a limited number of locations. Of the 500 or so places visited, I have selected those which I feel are the most interesting. My primary objective was to repeat the earlier picture as closely as possible, but inevitably there were problems in some cases. These ranged from construction of new buildings or other development, growth of trees and scrub, or where access would have been required to the lineside, which is no longer allowed. In a few other locations I have moved to a slightly different position, if this offered a more interesting view of the scene today.

My journeys have taken me from Margate in the east, to Padstow in the west, some 300 miles as the crow flies. For pictures in the dense railway network of the London area, the Travelcard has been a real boon — almost without exception I found the trains clean and punctual. Further afield I have generally had to use my car, not only to reach places now without a train service, but also in order to cover the ground in the time available. The car mileage involved worked out at just short of 6,000.

The exceptionally dull and murky weather we have endured this winter has not made photography easy. On the worst days in January, poor light made it a struggle to take pictures before 10am and after 2.30pm — often the brightest object I could see was the cheerful red LED display showing shutter speed and lens aperture data in the camera viewfinder! Even at Hastings in mid-March, on what had been a sunny day, mist suddenly rolled in from the sea, reducing visibility to a few yards. A repeat visit was required to obtain the pictures for the book.

I took some 1,200 photographs during my journeys, nearly all with a Canon A1 camera fitted with the standard Canon 50mm f1.4 lens. This excellent general purpose lens could cope with all but the most dismal conditions. The film used was Kodak T-Max 400 processed with T-Max developer – I printed the negatives on Kentmere Kenthene Glossy paper.

It has been a fascinating, if sometimes disheartening experience to re-visit locations I had not been to for as much as 35 years. I felt like a stranger from another time in some places — for instance at Wadebridge, roads and houses now covered the once familiar positions where I had photographed the Beattie Well Tanks.

Trying to discover old railway sites in a strange town, especially one where there have been no trains for some years, can be a daunting experience. Time is required to find the location and orientate oneself for the repeat picture. Passers-by have invariably been kind, interested and helpful; the sight of the old pictures often bringing back interesting memories and reminiscences of the railway as it used to be.

My wife, who accompanied me on most of my longer journeys, has been an enormous help, and my thanks are due to her. Apart from map reading, she soon became an expert at searching for tell-tale signs of closed stations (such as the indestructible 'Southern' concrete fence posts, or the ubiquitous 'Station Road'). She also organised accommodation and checked my

position and alignment for the 'Now' picture, against the old photograph. She has also provided invaluable assistance in going through my captions, as well as offering helpful and constructive comments on the book as it has taken shape.

There are others too who I would like to thank for their indispensable assistance – the photographers (in particular Colin Hogg and Brian Stephenson), who have kindly allowed me to draw on their splendid collections for the 'Then' pictures where my own has been lacking: Gerald Siviour for speeding the work by photographing some locations for me in Kent and East Sussex, notably on the KESR; Terry Gough for readily offering help and advice based on his own 'Then and Now' work; Roger Cruse for his interest and guidance; European Passenger Services for access to their offices at Waterloo to take a 'Now' picture; David Medhurst of Southern Track Renewals Company Ltd, and Malcolm Tomlin of Wessex Train Care Ltd, for arranging visits to the former steam locomotive works at Ashford and Eastleigh respectively.

The work in putting this large book together against a tight timescale would have come to nothing were it not for the efforts of the staff at Ian Allan Publishing and Printing. I am very grateful to them for their support, in particular Peter Waller, who, by writing the Preface on the Southern, has allowed me to concentrate on the pictures, and Nick Lerwill who has worked wonders with the production of the book.

Looking back on my odyssey round the 'Southern', some places inevitably stand out for one reason or another — for example a station may have been particularly impressive, another totally the opposite. BAFTA (the British Academy of Film and Television Arts) makes its awards, so why not some for *The Southern Then and Now*! For what they are worth, here are my categories, nominations and 'winners', drawn from the places depicted in the book: **Most Mourned Closed Location**, *Nominations:* Lyme Regis, Wadebridge, West Meon. *Winner:* Wadebridge; **Best Reopened Station**, *Nominations:* Corfe Castle, Kingscote, Medstead & Four Marks. *Winner:* Kingscote; **Special Winner for the most Promising Reopened Station:** Shepherds Well (East Kent Railway); **Best 'Now' British Rail Station**, *Nominations:* Axminster, Templecombe, Windsor & Eton Riverside; *Winner:* Windsor & Eton Riverside; **Worst 'Now' BR Station**, *Nominations:* Mitcham, Ore, St Budeaux (Victoria Road). *Winner:* Mitcham. **Best Closed Station**, *Nominations:* Ashey, Horsebridge, Tipton St John's. *Winner:* Horsebridge.

You probably won't agree with all of these choices, but thinking about your own preferences may add to the interest of the locations. I hope you enjoy the book.

Mike Esau
Richmond, Surrey
May 1996

Author Mike Esau

Bibliography

British Railways Maps and Gazetteer 1825 - 1985, C. J. Wignall, (Oxford Publishing Company)
British Railways Past and Present - Berkshire and Hampshire, Terry Gough, (Past and Present Publishing Ltd)
British Railways Past and Present - Surrey and West Sussex, Terry Gough, (Past and Present Publishing Ltd)
Bulleid's Pacifics, D.W.Winkworth, (George Allen and Unwin)
Kent Coast Heyday, Mike Esau and Gerald Siviour, (Ian Allan Ltd)
LSWR West Country Lines Then and Now, Mac Hawkins, (David &Charles)
Railways of the Southern Region, Geoffrey Body, (Patrick Stephens Limited)
Railways of the Western Region, Geoffrey Body, (Patrick Stephens Limited)
The Sidmouth, Seaton & Lyme Regis Branches, Maggs, Paye, (The Oakwood Press)
Waterloo-Exeter Heyday, Gerald Siviour and Mike Esau, (Ian Allan Ltd)

Preface

Although the Southern Railway was the smallest of the 'Big Four' railway companies established at the Grouping in 1923, it had a long history, with the first sections of route dating back to the early years of the 19th century as well as a fascinating record of innovation and progress. The new company was formed of three constituents — the London, Brighton & South Coast Railway, the London & South Western Railway and the South Eastern & Chatham Railway (the last-named representing an earlier amalgamation between the London, Chatham & Dover and the South Eastern railways). These railways passed on to the new Southern Railway both a complex network of suburban lines — a number of which were already electrified — serving south London alongside a comprehensive system of main and secondary routes that served the region. Of the three pre-Grouping companies the largest, with its long main lines to Weymouth and Exeter (with access to the 'Withered Arm' of lines in North Devon and Cornwall), was the LSWR; the smallest, concentrated in Kent, was the SECR.

The first line in the area was the Surrey Iron Railway, the first section of which opened in July 1803; this line now forms part of the still extant Wimbledon-West Croydon route. The Surrey Iron Railway was followed by the Canterbury & Whitstable, which opened in May 1830. This second historical line has fared less well, being closed completely in 1952. Two other pioneering lines followed: the London & Greenwich (opened in 1836) and the London & Croydon (opened in 1839). Both of these lines served London Bridge, although having separate stations; the former was to become part of the SECR and the latter part of the LBSCR. The next major entrant to the scene was the London & Southampton Railway (later to form the core of the LSWR) which opened from Nine Elms (on the approach to the later terminus at Waterloo) to Woking in 1838.

The London & Southampton became the London & South Western Railway in 1839 and its network expanded. Its line between Southampton and Winchester opened in the same year, whilst the completing link between Basingstoke and Winchester was opened the following year. The line to Portsmouth was opened in 1841, but was temporarily closed whilst a tunnel at Fareham was strengthened; the line reopened in 1842. The Woking-Guildford line was opened in 1845; Southampton-Dorchester via Ringwood (the 'Castleman's Corkscrew') line in 1847; Eastleigh-Salisbury in 1847; Nine Elms-Waterloo in 1848; Richmond-Datchet in 1848; Guildford-Ash Junction-Farnham in 1849; the Hampton Court branch in 1849; Farnham-Alton in 1852; Staines-Wokingham in 1856; Basingstoke-Andover in 1854; Andover-Salisbury in 1857; and the Lymington branch in 1858. Access to Exeter was finally gained in 1860.

Once the LSWR reached Exeter, it was able to capitalise upon its earlier (slightly suspect) acquisition of the Bodmin & Wadebridge Railway (which had opened originally in 1834). The next stage in the opening up of the 'Withered Arm' came with the leasing of the Exeter & Crediton Railway in 1862 (a line with which the LSWR had been controversially involved earlier) and the North Devon Railway & Dock Co the following year. From these lines the LSWR's empire in the West Country expanded; Okehampton was reached in 1867 and Lydford in 1874. The same year

(1874) saw the opening of the line from Barnstaple to Ilfracombe. For the next 20 years, LSWR metals continued to spread through the region, ultimately reaching Plymouth Friary in 1891, Bude in 1898 and Padstow the following year. At Barnstaple, the Lynton & Barnstaple line, opened in 1898, was the West Country's only 1ft 11.5in passenger line. Nominally independent, it entered into negotiations with the LSWR, but these were overtaken by the Grouping of 1923 and the L&BR lost its independence in July of that year.

The London, Brighton & South Coast Railway was the result of an amalgamation in 1846 between the London & Croydon and the London & Brighton railways. The latter was opened in stages during 1840/41 and prior to the merger with the L&CR, had already taken over the Brighton & Chichester Railway. The 1846 amalgamation also authorised the take-over of the Brighton, Hastings & Lewes Railway. Further extensions followed; these included: Chichester-Havant-Portsmouth in 1847; Lewes-Wivelsfield in 1847; Horsham-Three Bridges in 1848; the Eastbourne branch in 1848; Lewes-Uckfield in 1858; and, Horsham-Pulborough-Petworth in 1859. Victoria station was opened in 1860. Additional lines completed included: Christ's Hospital-Shoreham in 1861; Christ's Hospital-Guildford in 1865; Pulborough-Ford in 1863; the Littlehampton branch in 1863; East Grinstead-Tunbridge Wells in 1866; Horsham-Leatherhead in 1867; Uckfield-Tunbridge Wells in 1868; and Eridge-Polegate in 1880.

The third of the main constituents of the SR was the SECR. This was created in 1899 when the SECR and the LCDR pooled their management and operations, although the two companies were to retain their actual independence until 1923. The SER's main line, linking London with Dover, opened in stages between 1842 and 1844. Additional lines soon followed. These included: Maidstone-Paddock Wood (1844); Tonbridge-Tunbridge Wells (1845); Reading-Guildford-Reigate (1849); Ashford-Hastings (1851); Hastings-Tunbridge Wells (1852); Maidstone-Strood (1852); Ashford-Ramsgate-Margate (1856) and Lewisham-Beckenham (1857). The SER took over the operation of the pioneering London & Greenwich in 1845. Initially SER services terminated at Bricklayers Arms, but Charing Cross station was opened in 1864 and Cannon Street followed two years later.

The LCDR was a later company that emerged from the original East Kent Railway (not to be confused with the later East Kent Light Railway that built the line to the east of Shepherds Well). The EKR opened between Faversham and Strood in 1858, with the line to Canterbury opening slightly later. Authorisation to extend to Dover and a link with the earlier West End of London & Crystal Palace Railway brought a change of name, with it becoming the London, Chatham & Dover in August 1859. The LCDR reached Dover in 1861 and, via the Herne Bay & Faversham Railway (later renamed the Margate Railway), Herne Bay in 1861 and Margate/Ramsgate in 1863.

Physically separated from the mainland, but with almost as complex a railway history, was the network of lines built to serve the Isle of Wight. There were three independent companies on the island at the Grouping (the Isle of Wight Central Railway, the Freshwater, Yarmouth & Newport Railway and the Isle of Wight Railway) along with a short LSWR/LBSCR joint line (from St John's Road to Ryde Esplanade). The first section to open was that between Newport and Cowes in 1862. This was followed by Ryde St John's Road-Shanklin (1864) and Shanklin-Ventnor (1866). The last section of the Isle of Wight network to be completed was the line from

BOSCARNE JUNCTION

Then : April 1958
On this lovely spring morning, one of the Beattie Well Tanks is carrying out some shunting in the sidings at Boscarne Junction, before travelling up the china clay branch to Wenford Bridge. The line in front of the camera carried trains between Wadebridge and Bodmin. This divided at the junction into lines for Bodmin North (ex-LSWR), and Bodmin General (ex-GWR).

Merstone to St Lawrence (opened 1897) and thence to Ventnor (1900). The entire island network passed to SR control in 1923 and remained intact until Nationalisation; the first section to close being that between Merstone and Ventnor in 1952.

Both the LSWR and the LBSCR were amongst the first railway exponents of the use of electric traction in railway operation. The LBSCR adopted the 6,700V dc overhead system, the first sections of which were inaugurated between 1909 and 1912. The LSWR, in contrast, selected the 660V dc third-rail system, introducing its first services in 1915. The LBSCR electrified lines served routes out to Sutton and Coulsdon North; they were re-electrified by the Southern Railway to the third-rail scheme in the late 1920s. The initial LSWR scheme covered a number of suburban lines, including the Kingston and Hounslow loops and the Shepperton branch. The newly established SR was to extend the LSWR's scheme to include the lines to Dorking, via Leatherhead, and Guildford, via Claygate, between 1923 and 1925.

The Grouping of 1923 brought almost all the railways of southern England under single management for the first time; there were odd exceptions (such as the Kent & East Sussex and the East Kent railways), which only passed into Southern control at Nationalisation. The new Southern Railway continued its predecessors' policy of electrification, extending the electrification of the suburban lines but also, for the first time, bringing the third-rail on to the main lines. The 1930s were to witness the wholesale electrification of lines in east Hampshire and Sussex, with the completion of schemes for the Portsmouth and Brighton routes, the Sussex Coast line and the Littlehampton/Bognor Regis line. Elsewhere the Southern completed the final link in the Cornish network, with the opening of the Halwill Junction-Torrington line and continued with the construction of additional capacity in the suburban network (most obviously the Chessington South branch opened in 1938). These positive developments were, however, countered by less favourable aspects as the Southern, like all the other railway companies, grappled with the rise of road transport and the declining finances of certain lines. There were a number of closures during this period, most notably the narrow gauge Lynton & Barnstaple route in 1936.

As with the other 'Big Four' companies, the Southern Railway passed to the control of the British Transport Commission, as a constituent of British Railways, in 1948. Initially, there was to be little radical change in as much as the new Southern Region was effectively the old Southern Railway; anachronisms such as the 'Withered Arm', which would eventually pass to Western Region control, were not immediately removed, whilst locomotives of Southern Railway design continued to appear. Gradually, however, the new owners started to impose their own identity; although green was retained as the Southern's corporate colour, elsewhere 'British Railways' started to appear on the sides of locomotives and some of the traditional restrictions disappeared. The period of the 1950s witnessed a number of significant developments. Although few in comparison with the post-1960 era, there were line closures. Passenger lines to close during the period included the Port Victoria branch (1951), the Turnchapel branch (1951), the Bulford branch (1952), the Ventnor West branch (1952), the Gosport branch (1953), the Chichester-Midhurst line (1953), the Kent & East Sussex line (1954), the Crystal Palace (High Level) branch (1954), the Alton-Fareham line (1955), the Bordon branch (1956), the Lewes-Horsted Keynes line (1958) and the Melcombe Regis branch (1959).

Not all, however, was doom and gloom during the period. Towards the end of the decade the Kent Coast electrification scheme was designed to bring the third-rail to the main lines out of London to Dover, Folkestone, Maidstone and Ramsgate. Opened in stages between 1959 and 1967, the scheme eliminated much steam-hauled passenger services from the region's Eastern Section and allowed for the transfer of numerous locomotives to the Western Section. From one of the closures of the period — the much contested closure of the Horsted Keynes-Lewes line — emerged the first preservation scheme to attempt the reopening of an ex-British Railways standard gauge line — the Bluebell Railway. Now, almost 40 years on from closure, the Bluebell is turning back the clock of railway closures and reopening the line north to link in with services at East Grinstead.

As elsewhere on British Railways, the Beeching Report of 1963 foreshadowed many closures, although, with much of its track mileage devoted to commuter services into London, the Southern was to fare better than certain other regions. Despite this, there were to be a number of significant closures. Amongst lines proposed for closure were all those of the ex-LSWR's 'Withered Arm' in North Devon and Cornwall, with the exception of the line from Exeter to Barnstaple. Other lines that were threatened included Ashford-New Romney, Guildford-Horsham, Brockenhurst-Ringwood-Bournemouth, the branches to Lyme Regis, Sidmouth and Seaton and Romsey-Andover. A number of other lines that were proposed for closure were, however, to escape the 'axe'. These included Ashford-Hastings and the Exmouth branch. The mid-1960s onwards saw many of these closures take effect and, at the same time, familiar motive power was gradually to disappear. The ex-LSWR main line to Weymouth was the last steam-operated main line, but even here steam was to finally succumb, with Southern steam operation coming to an end in July 1967.

After the major closures of the Beeching era, the Southern Region entered a period of relative stability during the 1970s and early 1980s. There were odd closures (like the branch to Swanage and the Mid-Hants line from Alton to Winchester, both of which are now home to thriving preservation schemes), but the ex-LSWR main line west of Salisbury towards Exeter survived, although much reduced in status.

From the creation of Network SouthEast in 1986 the importance of the old Southern Region gradually declined. New initiatives, like the opening of Thameslink and the completion of electrification through to Weymouth, altered traditional traffic patterns and brought the possibility of new services. As elsewhere on British Rail, the mid to late 1980s saw improvements to finances and an optimism generated by the new business Sectors; an optimism that was to be overturned firstly by the decline in business caused by the recession at the end of that decade and then, just when business was starting to increase, by the doubts caused by the prospect of railway privatisation.

The new era dawned on 1 April 1995 when British Rail was divided into Railtrack and into the various Train Operating Units. Three major TOUs now serve the lines of the former Southern Region — South West Trains (now in the ownership of the bus company Stagecoach), Network SouthCentral (which is soon to pass to French control) and South East Trains — alongside two others (Gatwick Express and Thameslink) that also operate over erstwhile SR lines. It is ironic that the operations of the three major TOUs mirror considerably the services inherited by the Southern from the LSWR, the LBSCR and the SECR in 1923. In three-quarters of a century the Southern's lines have almost turned full circle.

BOSCARNE JUNCTION

Now : 15 September 1995

Though I did not know it at the time, this picture has proved ideal for use in the book. It was taken on the occasion of a charter freight on the Bodmin & Wenford Railway, whose headquarters are at the former GWR station at Bodmin General. By special arrangement, our freight train came down to the former Boscarne Junction, and here it is with '5700' class pannier tank No 7714, at the site of the old sidings. The crossing keeper's house in the background provides the obvious link between the two pictures. The Camel Trail runs alongside the line behind the fence on the right of the picture.
Both Author

1 CHARING CROSS (1)

Then : 21 April 1951

This early post Nationalisation picture shows St Leonards shed 'Schools' class No 30912 *Downside*. The photographer noted that the time was approximately 2.15pm, so the train is probably the 2.25pm departure to Hastings where it is scheduled to arrive at 4.19pm. To the right is SR suburban unit No S4249, and, crowning the station roof behind, the Southern Railway Coat of Arms.

Now : 26 January 1996

The station has been totally been redeveloped, though the building block style of architecture may not win universal approval. Happily the Coat of Arms and 'SR' have been incorporated into the new station, though I wonder how many travellers know what the letters stand for! Two Class 466 units wait to leave with services to the southeast London and Kent suburbs. *P. H. Wells/Author*

3 HUNGERFORD BRIDGE

Then : 2 October 1946

This view was taken from Waterloo station looking towards Charing Cross and the north bank of the Thames. Much bomb damage is still visible but the area was to be cleared for the 1951 Festival of Britain, and later, the Shell Centre. The almost new No 21C132 *Camelford*, (in traffic June 1946) but then unnamed, is passing with a Kent coast express.

2 CHARING CROSS (2)

Then : 1957
'Schools' class 4-4-0 No 30905 *Tonbridge* is arriving with a train from Hastings, whilst on the far right an Ivatt 2-6-2T waits to leave with empty stock. This picture shows the signalbox which straddled the tracks at the outer end of the station, and to the left is the old Shot Tower on the other side of the Thames.

Now : 26 January 1996
Almost 40 years on and the scene is very different, for modern signalling and point equipment has removed the need for the old manual box. This has opened up the view over Hungerford Bridge to reveal the Royal Festival Hall and the Shell Centre, where the flags on the roof stretch out in an icy easterly wind blowing snow flurries up the Thames. A Class 466 unit is arriving on a Kent suburban service. *N. C. Simmons/Author*

3 HUNGERFORD BRIDGE

Now : 23 November 1995
This is the nearest comparison picture I could manage since to have secured an exact copy I would have had to be suspended in mid-air! However, it shows the new Charing Cross station, the Royal Festival Hall (with the Post Office Tower poking above it) and the Shell Centre. Much of the bridgework is still the same, and the wall by the side of the road leading diagonally under the railway still survives. The unusual lack of traffic in York Road was due to a demonstrators march blocking Waterloo bridge — a hazard of modern times! *Courtesy National Railway Museum York/Author, Courtesy European Passenger Services*

4 WATERLOO JUNCTION (EAST)

Then : 9 September 1960

The Shell Centre on the South Bank is under construction in this picture showing Bricklayers Arms shed 'Schools' class 4-4-0 No 30927 *Clifton* calling at the station with the 11.46am Charing Cross to Ashford train. Platforms at Waterloo East are lettered A to D to avoid confusion with those on the main station to which it was once linked by a connecting line. The site of the junction can still be seen on the right hand side of the line on the approach to the station from Charing Cross.

Now : 7 March 1996

The Shell Centre dominates this view of Waterloo East where, apart from the removal of some of the platform canopies, the installation of modern lighting and CCTV equipment, little has changed. A 4-VEP unit is leaving the station with the 11.03 service to Ramsgate which it is due to reach at 13.19 via Ashford, Dover Priory and Deal.
J. Scrace/Author

5 CANNON STREET (1)

Then : 28 May 1953

Cannon Street station was opened by the South Eastern Railway on 1 September 1866, its outstanding feature being the 120ft high twin towers. The single arched roof of iron and glass between the towers miraculously survived the Blitz which devastated this part of London. On the bridge outside the station an ex-London Midland Region 2-6-2T is leaving with a train of empty stock and will shortly pass a Maunsell 2-6-0 and 'C' class 0-6-0. Barges are much in evidence on the river emphasising the importance of the London Docks at this time.

Now : 26 January 1996

Some 43 years later, the twin towers of the station, and St Paul's Cathedral behind, still dominate the scene, which is taken from London Bridge looking in a northwesterly direction. The space once occupied by the arch has been filled by new office accommodation. Much recent development is in evidence along the river front, and the barges have been replaced by a pleasure boat, reflecting the closure of the London Docks and the growth of business and tourism.
R. E. Vincent/Author

6 CANNON STREET (2)

Then : 31 August 1954
Moving further north across London Bridge this was the view looking west. 'D' class 4-4-0 moves out the station past the large signalbox, with the 9.52am Cannon Street to Grove Park empty stock train. Bankside power station on the south bank of the Thames is in operation, whilst to its right, the white bulk of Shell Mex House can be glimpsed through the haze.

Now : 26 January 1996
Bankside power station (due to become an extension of the Tate Gallery to display modern art) is still there, as is Shell Mex House. Other newer tall office buildings can be seen on the skyline, whilst on the river, a floating restaurant and a pleasure boat have replaced the barges. On the bridge a train for Dartford is leaving the station. *Colin Hogg/Author*

8 LONDON BRIDGE (2)

Then : 31 May 1961
In the last year or so of steam working, class 'E1' 4-4-0 No 31507 awaits departure from London Bridge with the 7.24am London Bridge to Ramsgate train. This service was a regular working for the speedy and efficient 'D1' or 'E1' class 4-4-0s right up to the end of steam. The train thus became a popular one with enthusiasts either to travel on or photograph from the lineside. The 'D1' and 'E1' loco-motives had a long and distinguished career on the main lines to the Kent coast and remained on important duties well after the arrival of the
Bulleid pacifics.

7 LONDON BRIDGE (1)

Then : 5 September 1960

On a sunny late summer evening, rebuilt Bulleid pacific No 34014 *Budleigh Salterton*, which was modified in March 1958, comes slowly round the sharp curve from Borough Market Junction into the station with the 6.21pm train from Cannon Street to Deal. This service was one of a number which ran for City office workers to and from Cannon Street in the morning and evening peak periods.

Now : 26 January 1996

Little remains of the 1960 buildings, and now new office development and the station control box dominate the picture. It shows a Cannon Street to London Bridge shuttle service, composed of a Class 466 EMU, arriving at the station. A link with the past is the warehouse on the right hand side of the picture which has been refurbished, possibly in connection with the tourist attractions which have been opened round the station in recent years, such as The London Dungeon. *Colin Hogg/Author*

8 LONDON BRIDGE (2)

Now : 22 January 1996

That nothing remains of the old station is clear from this picture taken in approximately the same position. London Bridge and its environs was resignalled and the tracks remodelled in the 1970s, the new station being completed in 1978. The old open footbridge has been replaced by a wide enclosed bridge which extends to the 'Brighton' side of the station. On the left of the picture is the tower of Guy's Hospital which dominates the view from the station looking north. *J. Scrace/Author*

9 ST JOHNS

Then : 10 June 1961

This station, opened in 1873, gained notoriety for being close to the scene of the Lewisham accident in 1957 (see Lewisham). The viaduct over the main line which was severely damaged in this accident, is clearly visible from its platforms. In this picture, looking in the other direction, 'Schools' class 4-4-0 No 30924 *Haileybury* is passing the main line platform with the 9.10am Charing Cross to Ramsgate train.

Now : 1 February 1996

The main line platform has now been removed leaving an island platform serving the Lewisham line. The station is linked to Cliff Terrace by a long new footbridge which offers splendid views of trains coming into London from the Orpington direction. The evening peak period is just getting underway with the 16.00 train from Charing Cross to Ramsgate passing the station. *J. Scrace/Author*

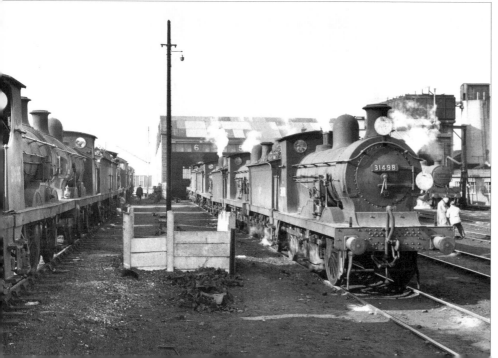

11 HITHER GREEN LOCOMOTIVE SHED

Then : 1959

Here is a fine line up of at least seven 'C' class 0-6-0s together with a glimpse of a 'W' class 2-6-4T on the right. The picture emphasises the role of the shed, which opened in 1933, in providing motive power for shunting in the adjacent marshalling yards and working transfer freights to other BR Regions in the London area.

10 LEWISHAM

Then : 7 September 1958

Something of the complexity of the lines at Lewisham is shown in this picture of Standard Class 5 No 73081 entering the Blackheath line platforms with a down boat train. The train will have come from Victoria via Peckham Rye, Nunhead and the Lewisham flyover, scene of the tragic accident on 4 December 1957 when Bulleid pacific No 34066 *Spitfire*, on a train from Cannon Street, ploughed into the back of a stationary electric train. No 73081 is carrying the Bexleyheath line disc code, so I think the train has been diverted due to engineering works on the main line.

Now : 1 February 1996

Electric multiple-unit No 466025 is entering this busy station with the 11.46 train from Victoria to Dartford which is following the same route as No 73081. The variety of warning signs and the unchecked growth of lineside trees is in contrast to the less cluttered nature of the earlier picture. *Colin Hogg/Author*

11 HITHER GREEN
LOCOMOTIVE SHED

Now : January 1996

Happily the shed survives though only three of the former six roads remain. It now houses a variety of freight locomotives and track maintenance vehicles. *Author/Gerald Siviour*

12 ELTHAM WELL HALL/ELTHAM

Then : 30 May 1959

'King Arthur' 4-6-0 No 30800 *Sir Meleaus de Lile* is pausing at Eltham Well Hall station with the 2.35pm Victoria to Ramsgate train which has been diverted via the Bexleyheath line due to engineering works. Eltham Well Hall and Eltham Park, only half a mile apart, have now been closed and a new station with bus interchange facilities built at Glenlea Road Eltham.

Now : 1 February 1996

Here is the new station at Eltham with a Class 465 EMU in the down side platform with a train for Dartford. The attractive new station buildings, car park and bus interchange are located at a lower level on the left hand side of the picture. *D. W. Winkworth/Author*

14 NEW ELTHAM

Then : c1958

One station further down the line is New Eltham where, possibly on the same day as the picture of No 31877 at Mottingham, Standard Class 5 No 73081 is passing with a diverted down train. Although the station building and bridges look grubby and work stained, the embankments are well kept and the lineside trees have been kept in check.

13 MOTTINGHAM

Then : c1958

Southernmost of the three principal lines linking Dartford with London is the route opened in 1866 which branches off at Hither Green and runs via Mottingham and Sidcup. This busy line is primarily for commuter services and did not see regular steam working after electrification. In this picture 'N1' class 2-6-0 No 31877 is passing the station with an unknown train, probably on a Sunday diversion. The disc code on the locomotive indicates that the train is travelling via the Dartford loop line.

Now : 1 February 1996

Most of the attractive wooden station buildings survive on the down side, though work has been carried out to modernise the canopies over the platforms which have new lighting. The signalbox and semaphore signals have long gone and the familiar green painted wooded slatted seats have been replaced by the red moulded metal type. These are more able to withstand the onslaught of vandalism, sadly so familiar today at stations in urban areas. The Class 465 unit is arriving with a train for Sidcup, and even in the off peak period the station is served by three trains an hour in each direction. *D. Lawrence/Author*

14 NEW ELTHAM

Now : 1 February 1996

As at Mottingham, the smartly painted wooden station buildings have survived on the down side. On the embankment, however, young saplings have been allowed to grow unchecked exacerbating the difficulties with leaf fall in the autumn which causes adhesion and braking problems on the new trains. A Class 466 unit has just arrived at the station with a service for Dartford. *D. Lawrence/Author*

15 ELMSTEAD WOODS

Then : 18 May 1956

'L' class 4-4-0 No 31765 is passing the station with the eight-coach 5.21pm train from Cannon Street to Faversham and Ramsgate, one of the evening services for City workers. The train has just emerged from Chislehurst tunnel with its two parallel bores serving the fast and slow lines. The station, which is located in a wooded cutting, retains much of its secluded and rural atmosphere.

Now : 1 February 1996

Whilst the basic structure of the station is the same, the platforms have been raised and TV monitors have been installed in connection with one man train operation. The attractive concrete fencing has been removed to reveal the cars of commuters from the surrounding residential areas. A Class 466 unit waits at the platform with a train from Charing Cross to Sevenoaks. *Colin Hogg/Author*

The station gardens on the island platform, complete with seats and a pond. *Author*

16 DUNTON GREEN (1)

Then : 28 October 1961

This was the station for the Westerham branch, which opened in 1881 and closed on 28 October 1961. On the last day of passenger working, 'H' class 0-4-4T No 31518, embellished with suitable chalk inscriptions, is coming through the station *en route* for Sevenoaks with empty stock from the branch. In the 1950s the branch enjoyed an approximately hourly service on Monday to Friday between the hours of 6am and 11pm.

Now : 23 February 1996

Speeding down the gradient from Polhill tunnel, a 4-VEP unit passes the station with the 11.00 service from Charing Cross to Ramsgate. Apart from the inevitable changes in signalling and platform equipment, the station has, on the face of it, changed little over the years. However, the view to the left of the picture where trains left for Westerham is very different as the following pictures show.
Colin Hogg/Author

17 DUNTON GREEN (2)

Then : 9 June 1959

On the up side of the line, 'H' class No 31239 waits to leave the bay platform on a summer evening with a train for Westerham. The train is composed of ex-SECR steam railmotor coaches. The four and three quarter mile journey over the branch will take but 11 minutes.

Now : 23 February 1996

The scene today is sadly one of dereliction for nothing remains of the bay platform. The trackbed of the branch curves away behind me and its course can be traced for a mile or so before it is lost under the M25.
D. M. C. Hepburne-Scott
(Rail Archive Stephenson)/Author

19 BRASTED

Then : c1961

Another two miles down the branch comes Brasted station which served the small village on the road from Westerham to Sevenoaks. Here 'H' class 0-4-4T No 31308 from Tonbridge shed has just left the station on its way to Westerham watched by a family enjoying a walk in the quiet lanes on the outskirts of the village. The sign below the embankment marks the drive that leads up to the station.

18 CHEVENING HALT

Then : 27 August 1961
This halt, one and quarter miles from Dunton Green, was the first stop on the branch. Not long before the line closed, 'H' class 0-4-4T No 31177, fitted with auto train equipment for push and pull working, is leaving the station with the 12.50pm train from Dunton Green to Westerham. As was usual on the branch, the locomotive is pulling the train to Westerham.

Now : 23 February 1996
Nothing remains of the branch at this point and the site has been cleared and bulldozed. However, to the right of the picture the trackbed can be seen passing through the line of bushes towards Dunton Green. To my left a minor road crosses the M25 and M26 as well as the A21(T) road to Hastings, offering a superb view of these busy trunk routes.
J. Scrace/Author

19 BRASTED

Now : 23 February 1996
How the scene has changed today! Instead of an 'H' class pottering along the branch, the notoriously busy M25 now runs along the trackbed of the branch at this point. The small road on the right leads to a yard close up against the motorway. *Brian Stephenson/Author*

20 WESTERHAM

Then : 8 October 1961

The station was situated adjacent to the A233 road to Biggin Hill on the north side of the town. 'H' class 0-4-4T No 31530 has just arrived at the station on this sunny autumn afternoon. With only a few weeks to go before closure, the neat SER-built station is already beginning to show signs of neglect as the covering on the west end of the platform canopy is starting to come adrift. After closure of the line there were plans to preserve it but unfortunately these came to nothing.

Now : 23 February 1996

Apart from the railway cottages which can be seen behind the signalbox in the previous picture, little remains to remind the visitor that a branch terminus once stood in this area. Light industry has taken over the site and the indentation in the A233 road on the left hand side of the picture marks the former position of the entrance to the station.
Brian Stephenson/Author

22 TONBRIDGE (1)

Then : 12 April 1961

'Schools' 4-4-0 No 30924 *Haileybury* slowly pulls into the yard on the west side of the station with a freight train which consists mainly of empty coal wagons. Even at this date so close to the end of steam on the South Eastern section, it was quite unusual to see the 'Schools' class on a freight train, such workings generally being entrusted to Maunsell 'N' class 2-6-0s. If the disc code carried by the locomotive is to be believed, the train has probably come off the Hastings line. Hidden in the background by the yard is the direct line to London via Sevenoaks brought into use in 1868, thus obviating the need for all trains to travel on the original route through Redhill.

21 SEVENOAKS

Then : 1959

After a spell of duty on the Westerham branch, 'H' class No 31520 is seen entering the down main line platform at Sevenoaks with a train for Tonbridge composed of SECR steam railmotor coaches. On the platform a porter is loading some small items of merchandise on to his luggage trolley. Note the gas lamps hanging from the SR concrete lamp standard. The signals to the right of the locomotive control trains on the line to Otford and Swanley Junction.

Now : 23 February 1996

Apart from alterations to the platform lighting and signalling, little has changed over the intervening years. Unit No 1575 is entering the station with the 11.30 train from Charing Cross to Dover Priory. *Both Author*

22 TONBRIDGE (1)

Now : 13 February 1996

Superficially not a great deal has changed over the years, though the demise of wagon load freight is evident from the deserted nature of the yard. However, the sharp curve on the Sevenoaks line at the west end of the station has been eased and the track realigned over the years, most recently in connection with the commencement of Channel Tunnel services. In the yard Pullman liveried Class 73 No 73101 awaits its next turn of duty, whilst on the main line a two-car EMU, converted for crew training purposes, begins the climb to Sevenoaks. *Colin Hogg/Author*

23 TONBRIDGE (2)

Then : 12 April 1961

Taken from the bridge outside the station looking east, this picture shows 'U1' class 2-6-0 No 31901 arriving with a local train from Ashford. To the left of the picture is the extensive goods depot, whilst in the background on the right is the locomotive shed (74D) which had an allocation of about 50 locomotives in the 1950s including many pre-Grouping types. Just beyond the signalbox, where a Hastings diesel unit is standing, the line from Tunbridge Wells Central comes in from the right.

Now : 13 February 1996

Some 35 years later the goods depot has been replaced by a large car park, whilst the area formerly occupied by the motive power depot is given over to light industry. Approaching the station at speed over the simplified track layout is the 12.13 Eurostar service from Paris Nord to Waterloo where it is due to arrive at 14.13. *Colin Hogg/Author*

25 EDENBRIDGE

Then : 1958

Situated on an embankment to the north of the town, Edenbridge station, like Penshurst, also had staggered platforms as can be seen in this picture. 'H' class No 31523 is arriving with a stopping train for Redhill consisting of a three-coach SECR 'Birdcage' set. A train for Tonbridge, also composed of a 'Birdcage' set, has just stopped at the other platform. A little to the west of the station the line crosses the ex-LBSCR route from Oxted which has a station at Edenbridge Town (see page 101).

24 PENSHURST

Then : 1958
This station was on the original 1842 SER route from Redhill to Tonbridge. In the 1950s the passenger services on this line consisted mainly of local stopping services but regular through Kent coast to Birmingham and Birkenhead trains were routed this way. In this picture 'H' class 0-4-4T No 31310 on a train for Redhill, has just come through the 78yd long Penshurst tunnel prior to stopping at the station.

Now : 23 February 1996
New fencing round the station has prevented me from standing in the same position as the 1958 picture. This view is taken from the new footbridge and shows the 13.53 train from Maidstone West arriving at the station. The original Tonbridge bound platform has been dismantled and re-sited opposite the one for Redhill. *Both Author*

25 EDENBRIDGE

Now : 23 February 1996
Unlike Penshurst, Edenbridge station retains its staggered platforms though the old wooden buildings on the Tonbridge bound side have been demolished. Once again I have been unable to take my comparison picture from rail level but the higher position on the new footbridge does offer a better view of the modern station. A 4-VEP unit is arriving with a train from Maidstone West. *Both Author*

26 PADDOCK WOOD

Then : 1961
This picture is taken from the down main line platform looking east towards Ashford. 'Q1' class 0-6-0 No 33028 is arriving in the up main line platform with a local train from Maidstone West to Tonbridge, whilst 'H' class No 31308 shunts carriages for a train to Hawkhurst. Electric services have not yet commenced though the conductor rail is in place and the platform is being raised and extended.

Now : 13 February 1996
Whilst the bay platform on the down side of the station has been removed, this view is essentially the same as before. Once a busy centre for freight traffic, industry here is now almost completely served by road, obviating the need for the goods sidings that can be seen in the distance on the earlier photograph. Eurostar services achieve their fastest point to point timings this side of the Channel on this straight $26\frac{1}{2}$ mile section between Ashford to Tonbridge. A Eurostar service from Brussels is speeding through the station.
Both Author

27 HORSMONDEN

Then : 1960

The Hawhurst branch left the main line at Paddock Wood and ran for 11½ miles though lovely Wealden country to the terminus at Gills Green, some distance north of the town on the road to Cranbrook. The branch opened through to Hawkhurst in 1893 and closed completely on 10 June 1961. In its last years the branch was worked by 'H' class 0-4-4Ts and 'C' class 0-6-0s from Tonbridge shed such as No 31244. The engine has left the wagon and brake van it has brought from Hawkhurst in the platform. The guard is carrying the key to unlock the ground frame to allow No 31244 access to the yard. The oast houses on the right are a reminder of the importance of hop growing in this area.

Now : 13 February 1996

The station has now been taken over by the Old Station Garage and links with the past are the survival of the station building and the oast houses. *Both Author*

Inset

A close-up of the old station seen from the entrance side on 13 February 1996. *Author*

28 HAWKHURST

Then : 10 June 1961
The scene at Hawkhurst on the last day of regular passenger working. 'C' class 0-6-0 No 31588, complete with wreath over the buffer beam, has just arrived from Paddock Wood and enthusiasts are taking their last pictures. Are you among them? In the distance, by the side of the run round loop, is the signalbox, whilst the extensive goods yard is out of sight behind the station building.

Now : 14 February 1996
The station site is now owned by the Kent Woodware Co Ltd who have been specialists in wood turnery since the early years of this century. Happily the company have preserved the station signalbox and goods shed which can be seen in this picture on the left hand side and right of centre respectively.
Both Author

Inset
A close up view of the signalbox on 14 February 1996. *Author*

29 YALDING

Then : 14 August 1970

This station on the SER line from Paddock Wood to Maidstone West, was opened in 1844. At the time of this picture it was fully manned with a signalbox to control the traditional level crossing gates. Unit No 6065 is calling at the station with the 14.11 service from Strood to Paddock Wood.

Now : 13 February 1996

Compared with the neat and ordered scene of 26 years before, the station now presents a rather neglected appearance, and the old level crossing gates have been replaced by automatic lifting barriers. A 4-VEP unit is pausing briefly at the station with the 10.20 service from Maidstone West. *J. Scrace/Author*

30 WATERINGBURY

Then : 1961
Towards the end of steam in this area of Kent, 'Q1' class 0-6-0s from Tonbridge shed frequently worked trains over this line. Here No 33037 is arriving at the station with a service from Paddock Wood. The line is a picturesque one offering fine vistas over the River Medway which it follows much of the way to Maidstone.

Now : 13 February 1996
Unlike Yalding, Wateringbury retains its signalbox, semaphore signals and traditional level crossing gates. On this rather murky day, so typical of the winter of 1996, Unit No 1557 is arriving with the 10.53 train from Paddock Wood. *Both Author*

No visit to the station would be complete without a picture of the striking station building located on the Maidstone-bound platform, even if it is rather marred by the unsympathetic waiting shelter. *Author*

31 HEADCORN (1)

Then : 1961

Headcorn was the junction for the Kent & East Sussex Railway, opened to this point in 1905 and closed in January 1954. The bay platform for the KESR is out of sight to the left of this picture. 'Schools' class No 30934 *St Lawrence* is passing the station with a summer Saturday through train from the Midlands to the Kent coast. The original SER buildings on the down platform survived at this time.

Now : February 1996

Whilst the through lines have been retained and upgraded in connection with the Channel tunnel services, the old station building and footbridge have been replaced. Unusually a Eurostar service for Paris is passing the station on the down slow line possibly due to a points problem brought on by the snowy conditions.
Author/Gerald Siviour

32 HEADCORN (2)

Then : May 1954

In the bay platform the KESR line train waits to leave with the 12.30pm departure to Rolvenden consisting of 'O1' class 0-6-0 No 1434 hauling an ex- LSWR corridor coach. The train would take a leisurely 45 minutes to cover the 9½ to Rolvenden.

Now : 23 September 1995

Since the old KESR platform has been totally obliterated to make way for a new up relief line, the 'Now' picture from the same position would only show scrub and the high wire fence bordering the railway. I therefore thought it would be more interesting to include a picture of a main line steam train passing the site of the KESR line platform. This is the view looking towards Ashford, and the KESR line once curved away to the right of the picture. A hot air balloon is in the sky on this fine still evening above rebuilt to 'Merchant Navy' pacific No 35028 *Clan Line* which is using the new line with a 'Golden Arrow' Pullman train. It has made its way round Kent via Canterbury East and Dover and is returning to Victoria.

Ian Allan Library/Author

33 TUNBRIDGE WELLS CENTRAL/TUNBRIDGE WELLS (1)

Then : 1960

Situated on the line to Hastings, this station was opened in 1846, and is located in the centre of the town as its name implies. 'Q1' 0-6-0 No 33036, working an up freight train, is about to enter Wells tunnel which commences at the Tonbridge end of the station. The line drops steeply all the way to Tonbridge which, in the days of loose-coupled freight trains, called for good co-ordination between the driver and guard to ensure the speed of the descent was properly controlled.

Now : 13 February 1996

Despite the passing of the years, Tunbridge Wells retains most of its pleasing features including the fine station buildings. With the closing of Tunbridge Wells West (see page 105), the station has lost its 'Central' title. On the down line, unit No 1571 is waiting to leave with the 13.06 train to Victoria via Redhill. *Both Author*

The imposing clocktower on the down side of the station. *Author*

34 TUNBRIDGE WELLS CENTRAL/TUNBRIDGE WELLS (2)

Then : 1957
Shortly after leaving the station the line to Tunbridge Wells West veers off to the right at Grove Junction. 'H' class 0-4-4T No 31544 is arriving with a push and pull train from Tunbridge Wells West to Tonbridge. Further down the platform, 'L' class 4-4-0 No 31771 is waiting to leave with a stopping train to Brighton via Eridge. Note the smart double-deck bus passing over the road bridge.

Now : 13 February 1996
The station is now signalled for bi-directional working. On the London-bound side, unit No 1809 is leaving with the 13.04 service to Hastings, whilst at the other platform is the 12.53 arrival from Victoria via Redhill which terminates here. *Both Author*

36 ROBERTSBRIDGE

Then : September 1957
Robertsbridge was the western terminus of the Kent & East Sussex Railway, opened in 1900, which ran along the Rother valley to Rolvenden. By the time this picture was taken, normal passenger services over the line had been withdrawn. However, the line remained open as far as Tenterden for goods traffic and the occasional hop pickers special. Here ex-LBSCR 'Terrier' class 0-6-0T No 32678 from St Leonards shed, waits to leave the bay platform with a short hop pickers train for Northiam. By the look of it some of the local lads are hoping for a free ride! Happily No 32678 escaped scrapping and is currently undergoing restoration at Rolvenden.

35 WADHURST

Then : 1958

Carrying the same '22' headcode used by present day electric units, one of the Hastings line narrow-bodied diesel-electric units which were introduced in 1957, climbs the 1 in 80 gradient through the station with a train for Hastings. Just to the south of the station the line drops through the 1,205yd long Wadhurst tunnel, which marks the beginning of a long descent to the outskirts of Robertsbridge some 10 miles further on.

Now : 13 February 1996

The platform's attractive canopy has survived, though the loading dock has gone. The 15.21 semi-fast train to Cannon Street is leaving the station which the digital clock shows to be a trifle late. Modification work on the narrow tunnels, carried out when the line was electrified, now allows standard width stock to use the line. *Both Author*

36 ROBERTSBRIDGE

Now : February 1996

The bay platform still survives though the goods yard has been replaced by the now obligatory car park. There are plans to reopen the line from Robertsbridge to Bodiam which is the present limit of the preserved Kent & East Sussex Railway. Whether this goal will be achieved, only time will tell. A new footbridge links the two platforms, replacing the one situated at the north end of the station. *Author/Gerald Siviour*

37 BODIAM

Then : August 1953
In the last summer before closure of this section of the line to passenger traffic, 'Terrier' 0-6-0T No 32655 has arrived at the station with the 12.20pm train from Robertsbridge. Judging by the activity on the platform and the guard walking towards the front of the train with his shunting pole, it looks as if some wagons are to be detached. No 32655, like most of the 'Terriers' working at this time, was saved from cutting up on withdrawal from service. It is now based on the Bluebell Railway where it is better known by its original LBSCR name of *Stepney*.

Now : February 1996
Miraculously Bodiam station has remained unaltered over the years and is in course of restoration. This is the westernmost point of the Kent & East Sussex Railway today, though trains run no further than Northiam for the present. The station is well situated for the nearby Bodiam Castle.
G. F. Bannister/Gerald Siviour

39 ROLVENDEN

Then : 28 November 1953
The 8.50am mixed train from Headcorn is shunting at the station, before leaving for Robertsbridge where it is due at 10.31am. The shed is on the left of the picture, and the level crossing on the main road from Tenterden to Rolvenden is in the background to the rear of the brakevan.

38 NORTHIAM

Then : September 1957
This is the next station from Bodiam along the Rother Valley. 'Terrier' No 32678, a type synonymous with this section of the line, has just arrived with a hop pickers special train, though there do not seem to be any takers on this quiet Sunday evening. The locomotive will run round the train, and then return to Robertsbridge where a connection will be made with a service to London.

Now : February 1996
Northiam, the current the limit of operations on the KESR, remains substantially the same as it was in the 1950s, though the buildings and platform have been extended. A few years ago the station achieved some fame when it featured in a 'Challenge Anneka' television programme. The station was officially reopened by the Duke of Gloucester. *Author/Gerald Siviour*

39 ROLVENDEN

Now : February 1996
The KESR locomotive shed and workshop is located at Rolvenden and can be seen to the right of centre in this picture which is taken from the signalbox. The railway's Norwegian 2-6-0 is just about to leave the station with a train for Northiam.
N. Sprinks/Gerald Siviour

40 TENTERDEN TOWN/TENTERDEN

Then : 2 January 1954

It is the last day of passenger operation over the line, and 'O1' class 0-6-0 No 31065 is pulling out of the station with the 9.38am train to Robertsbridge which left Headcorn at 8.50am. Much of the delightful light railway atmosphere of this line, built by Colonel Stephens, comes over in this picture. No 31065 was not cut up when withdrawn, and after spending some time at the one-time preservation site in the old engine shed at Ashford, has now been dismantled.

Now : February 1996

The first section of the preserved railway was reopened from Tenterden on 3 February 1974. The station buildings remain almost unchanged, but the lovely three-arm semaphore signal has gone. Many more trains now run than in the days before closure, so a signalbox has been constructed to control traffic on what is now a busy line. Behind the signalbox is the new carriage shed and workshop.
Colin Hogg/Gerald Siviour

41 TENTERDEN ST MICHAELS TUNNEL

Then : 28 December 1953

One mile north of Tenterden Town station a small halt was constructed to serve a suburb of the town. Nearby lay the short St Michaels tunnel set in a wooded cutting. One of the regular 'O1' class 0-6-0s which worked the line in its last days, No 31065 from Ashford shed, coasts out of the tunnel towards the Town station with the 12.30pm train from Headcorn.

Now : February 1996

The photographer has struggled through fallen trees and dense undergrowth of almost Amazonian proportions to secure this picture of the south portal of the tunnel. There are no plans to restore services over this section of the line. *Colin Hogg/Gerald Siviour*

42 HIGH HALDEN ROAD

Then : 2 January 1954

On the last day of passenger services, 'O1' No 31065 pauses at High Halden Road at around 9.20 on this bright winter morning with the 8.50am train from Headcorn. The guard, who is standing in front of the official closure notice, has allowed the photographer a few moments to take his photograph.

Now : February 1996

Incredibly the station survives as a farm store and can clearly be seen from the A262 road between Biddenden and Tenterden which the line crossed at this point.
Colin Hogg/Gerald Siviour

43 BATTLE

Then : 9 September 1956
Not long before the introduction of the Hastings diesels to the line, 'Schools' class 4-4-0 No 30901 *Winchester* passes the station with the 4.50pm train from Hastings to Charing Cross. On Saturdays and Sundays this was a semi-fast train only calling at principal stations to Tunbridge Wells Central, and took just under two hours to reach Charing Cross. The equivalent Saturday train today is only about 20 minutes faster though it calls at more stations.

Now : 17 March 1996
Sunday engineering work is being carried entailing single line working, so the 15.26 departure to Charing Cross has just crossed over from the down line to stop at the station. Obvious changes from the earlier picture are the extension to the platform, the removal of the goods sidings, and the demolition of the platform canopy on the Hastings bound side of the station. *R. C. Riley/Author*

Battle station is a listed building and it is easy to see why from this picture of the frontage. *Author*

44 CROWHURST

Then : c1954

Crowhurst in the days when it was a busy junction for the Bexhill West branch opened in 1902. On the left a train from Charing Cross to Hastings, hauled by 'Schools' class 4-4-0 No 30900 *Eton*, is drawing to a halt to make a connection with the branch train on the right. This consists of a push and pull set which will be propelled to Bexhill West by an 'H' class 0-4-4T.

Now : 17 March 1996

The branch closed in June 1964 so the bay is now disused. With the decline in the importance of the station, the buildings have been removed, as well as the two through roads which can be seen in the earlier picture. Today the station only serves the small village nearby and is lightly used. *Ian Allan Library/Author*

45 SIDLEY

Then : 1957
Sidley is on the northern outskirts of Bexhill and was the only station on the branch to Bexhill West. The usual method of operation was for the 'H' class tank to propel its train to Bexhill as shown in this picture.

Now : 17 March 1996
The site of the station is now road maintenance materials yard. Since this was a Sunday I was unable to gain access to the yard, so have had to take this 'Now' picture, looking towards Bexhill, from the road overbridge which spans the end of the yard. *Both Author*

46 BEXHILL WEST

Then : 1958
The LBSCR station at Bexhill Central is located about a mile east of the terminus at Bexhill West. Both stations offered a service to London — for example in 1952 by leaving the West station on the 7am service, one could be in Cannon Street at 8.47am with a change at Crowhurst. On the Brighton line, the 7.3am train from the Central did not arrive at Victoria until 9.8am though the passenger could enjoy travel in a Pullman car on the electric service. Here 'H' class No 31519 waits to leave the station for Crowhurst. To the right is one of the then new Hastings diesel units.

47 WEST ST LEONARDS

Then : 4 August 1951

Immediately after the 1,318yd long Bopeep tunnel, the line to Tunbridge Wells leaves the coastal route to Eastbourne, before reaching West St Leonards station which is situated on a sharp curve. The 'Schools' class, such as No 30933 *King's Canterbury*, was the principal motive power for most passenger trains over the Hastings line. The locomotive is drawing to a halt with the 5.10pm train to Charing Cross which called at all stations to Tunbridge Wells Central.

Now : 15 May 1996

West St Leonards is an immaculately kept station which has recently been repainted in the 'South Eastern' house style. The 15.11 train from Hastings to Charing Cross is entering the up platform. It is particularly pleasing to record that the signal box at Bopeep Junction appears to be in as good a condition as it did all those years before.
B.C.Bending/Author

46 BEXHILL WEST

Now : 15 May 1996

The station building is now owned by Gorringes Auction Galleries. Their premises incorporate the canopies which were joined on to the rear of the station building - they can be seen above the first coach of the train in the 1958 picture. The remainder of the station site, including the former platform area, is now an industrial estate. Because of the new development it was impossible to stand in the same position as the earlier picture. This view is taken to the right and slightly further forward, but does give a good impression of what remains at the rear of the station.
Both Author

48 HASTINGS

Then : 24 April 1957

The view from the station looking towards St Leonards. 'L1' class 4-4-0 No 31757 is arriving with a stopping train from Tonbridge. The station, which was used by both SER and LBSCR trains in pre-Grouping days, was rebuilt by the Southern Railway in 1931 in its typical clean cut and modest style. The imposing viaduct in the background in fact only carries a secondary road over the tracks, but provides a fine vantage point to watch trains entering and leaving the station.

Now : 15 May 1996

The most obvious changes are the removal of the sidings and the replacement of the semaphore signals by colour lights. The train is the 11.48 through service from Brighton to Ashford composed of diesel electric unit No 207202 *Brighton Royal Pavilion*. At the time of writing, there are three trains on Monday to Saturday in each direction between Brighton and Ashford. These take about two hours for the sixty seven and a half mile journey. *J.N.Faulkner/Author*

49 ORE

Then : 6 September 1969

Ore is the first station out of Hastings on the line to Ashford opened by the SER in 1851. Mount Pleasant tunnel can just be seen in the background of this picture which shows diesel unit No 1001 calling at the station with the 1.11pm train from Hastings to Ashford. The conductor rail ends here, and behind the train is the depot once used for maintaining the stock built for the new 1935 electric service over the line from Victoria to Hastings via Lewes.

Now : 15 May 1996

No passengers were waiting to join diesel electric unit No 207201 *Ashford Fayre* forming the 12.24 train from Hastings to Ashford. The former electric depot is now disused, its neglected condition adding to the sense of better days past, at this now unmanned station. *J.Scrace/Author*

The eerie interior of the abandoned electric train depot on 15 May 1996. *Author*

50 DOLEHAM HALT/DOLEHAM

Then : 1958

When this picture was taken of an Ashford to Hastings train, the Standard Class 2 2-6-2Ts had only recently arrived on the Southern Region. The modern No 84023 is hauling an ancient two-coach LBSCR push and pull set which were always easily distinguishable by their prominent brass handrails. At this time the line was still double track throughout.

Now : February 1996

The Hastings to Ashford line has been partially singled in recent years as an economy measure. Diesel unit No 207202 is arriving at the station with a train from Ashford. The basic weekday service is hourly, plus three trains in each direction to Brighton. However, it seems the Brighton trains have not been a success and they are to be withdrawn. *Author/ Gerald Siviour*

52 RYE

Then : 1957

Some trains on the Ashford to Hastings lines terminated at Rye and this is such a working. 'H' class 0-4-T No 31295 has run round its coaches before returning to Hastings.

Now : February 1996

Because part of the line has been singled, Rye station is a now a passing place. Diesel unit No 207202, forming the 11.24 train from Hastings, has just arrived with a useful compliment of passengers. It has passed the 11.22 service from Ashford which is standing at the platform behind the photographer.
Author/ Gerald Siviour

51 WINCHELSEA

Then : 1957

The station is situated outside the town on the levels surrounding the River Brede. No 42095, one of the Fairburn 2-6-4Ts allocated to the Southern Region, bustles into the neatly kept platform with a train from Ashford.

Now : February 1996

What a sad contrast with the previous picture. The line is single, and the station facilities have been reduced to a small shelter, whilst the old level crossing has been replaced by flashing lights to warn of the approach of a train.
Author/Gerald Siviour

53 NEW ROMNEY

Then : c1954
The line from Lydd to New Romney closed in 1967. The terminus was adjacent to the Romney, Hythe & Dymchurch Railway which is located just out of sight on the right hand side of the picture. 'H' class 0-4-4T No 31512 is waiting to leave the station for the 22-mile run to Ashford via Lydd and Appledore.

Now : February 1996
No trace now remains of the station though the RHDR is happily still with us. However, with the closure of the branch, the RHDR can no longer be reached directly by rail.
Ian Allan Library/Gerald Siviour

55 MARTIN MILL

Then : 4 September 1968
Martin Mill is a somewhat bleak station situated on the lengthy climb from Deal through Walmer to the 1,412yd long Guston tunnel where the line drops down steeply to Dover. In this picture green painted electric multiple-unit No 6155 calls at the station with the 11.10am service from Margate to Charing Cross.

54 DEAL

Then : 9 September 1969

Deal was originally the terminus on the branch from Minster which opened in 1847, and it remained so until 1881 when the joint SER/LC&D line to Martin Mill and Dover came into use. The line approaches the town across the flat Lydden valley and, unlike other stations in this remote part of east Kent such as Sandwich and Ramsgate, Deal station is well situated in the centre of the town and close to the sea. In this picture the 14.05 Ramsgate to Charing Cross train is waiting to leave for Dover.

Now : 21 January 1996

Some rationalisation of the station layout and facilities has taken place in the intervening years. The buildings on the Ramsgate-bound platforms have been removed as has the centre line through the platforms. Otherwise much is the same including the ageing electric multiple-units, though these have been refurbished in recent years. Unit No 1595 is about to leave the station with the 13.02 train to Charing Cross where it is due to arrive at 15.07. *J. Scrace/Author*

55 MARTIN MILL

Now : 21 January 1996

A cold northerly wind is sweeping across the chalk downland as a four-car unit comes to a halt at the station with the 12.11 train to Charing Cross. The lighting has been modernised and the attractive old wooden canopy replaced by a new structure. Inside the station building the booking office is of particular interest since it also houses the signalbox. *J. Scrace/Author*

56 DOVER (1)

Then : 2 July 1956

Dover shed had an allocation of small locomotives for dock and quayside shunting including some of the useful 'P' class 0-6-0Ts, though ex-LSWR 'B4' class 0-4-0T No 30084 was the only member of its type at Dover. Here the 'B4' is on a typical duty bringing a wagon along Dover promenade towards the Western Docks, past a prewar Morris car which contrasts with the then modern Morris 1000 behind it.

Now : 22 January 1996

40 years on and there has been little change to the surroundings. The rails have gone though a hint of their outline can still be detected in the road. The quayside crane is still in position and the elegant buildings further down the promenade look almost the same — no smoke from passing locomotives now tarnishes their whiteness! The tall masts of the yachts in the marina on the other side of the bushes reflect the more affluent times we live in.
John Head/Author

57 DOVER (2)

Then : 8 August 1953
Just before 4pm, Class N No 31848 is passing Dover shed and Archcliffe Junction for the line to the Marine station, with the afternoon mail train from Ramsgate to Cannon Street (via Redhill), where it will not arrive until almost 7pm. In 1953 Dover shed (74C) had an allocation of some 50 locomotives. Of interest in this picture are the LBSCR 'E5' class 0-6-2T at the side of the shed (probably No 32593 on stationery boiler duties), and the 'P' class 0-6-0T as yard pilot beyond.

Now : 22 January 1996
No trace now remains of the shed, and with the closure of the Marine station and the cessation of the Dover — Dunkirk train ferry just before this picture was taken, there is no traffic to use the yard. The one-time Lord Warden Hotel in the background survives, though now used as office accommodation. An EMU is passing the junction with a train for Charing Cross. *W. Hamilton/Author*

58 DOVER (3)

Then : 14 June 1959
Stage 1 of the Kent Coast Electrification covering the Chatham route lines came into operation over the weekend of 13-14 June 1959. In this picture an Ivatt 2-6-2T No 41312, a few of which worked in Kent in the years leading up to electrification, pauses between shunting duties by the large signalbox controlling the entrance to Dover Marine station.

Now : 22 January 1996
Sadly Dover Marine (as Dover Western Docks) station closed in 1994, its fine architecture and atmospheric interior perhaps not being fully appreciated until the last days. I have adopted a slightly different viewpoint to show the full extent of the signal-box and the imposing entrance to the station. *Colin Hogg/Author*

59 DOVER (4)

Then : 1958

A view of the Western Docks and the Admiralty Pier from the heights of Shakespeare Cliff looking in an easterly direction. The shed is visible in the centre of the picture together with the sidings on reclaimed land used for storing coal wagons. A Standard class 2-6-4T is about to enter the 1,387yd long Shakespeare tunnel with a local train for Folkestone and Ashford.

Now : 22 January 1996

For this present day view I have had to move to the right slightly because of the erection of high fencing bordering the path up the cliffs. The housing at the top left of the picture remains much as before, though these properties now face the new A20(T) road which provides fast access to the Eastern Docks from the M20. In the background the one-time Lord Warden Hotel survives but the shed has gone. Behind the hotel are the greatly enlarged Eastern Docks, terminal for the cross-channel roll-on/roll-off ferry services. Four Class 47 locomotives, used for freight train haulage, are leaving the now empty yard where they have come to refuel, *en route* for Dollands Moor. *Both Author*

61 FOLKESTONE (1)

Then : 31 July 1955

Unrebuilt 'Battle of Britain' pacific No 34076 *41 Squadron* has just passed Folkestone Junction station with a train for London and is crossing the double arch bridge where the roads to Dover and Canterbury separate. Today the A259 road has been replaced by the new A20(T) trunk road which links Dover with the M20. Quite apart from the train, the road vehicles and advertisement hoardings add much interest to this picture.

60 FOLKESTONE HARBOUR

Then : 1959

Ex-Great Western Railway pannier tanks arrived at Folkestone in early 1959 to replace the 'R1' class 0-6-0Ts which had been used for many years to haul boat trains up the 1 in 30 gradient from the Harbour to Folkestone Junction station (closed in September 1965). In this picture two pannier tanks are setting out from the Harbour station, with a train of Bulleid and BR Mk1 stock, assisted by two other pannier tanks at the rear of the formation.

Now : 13 September 1991

In September 1991 steam returned when rebuilt Bulleid pacific No 34027 *Taw Valley* and BR Standard tank No 80080 made trips up and down the branch. Just as the 'R1s' and pannier tanks did for so many years up to 1961, the pacific gets hold of its train for the steep climb to the main line, assisted in the rear by the Standard tank whose steam can be seen to the left of the control tower. This part of the harbour has changed little over the years, but the increase in the number of boats reflects the growth of the leisure industry and the higher level of disposable income compared to the 1950s. *Both Author*

61 FOLKESTONE (1)

Now : 22 January 1996

The scene today is much the same though the hoardings have gone as well as the attractive road signs above the arches. To my right is the road leading to the Folkestone Harbour branch which it parallels down the hill, whilst the new road sign pointing to 'Tourist Information' and 'Pleasure Beach' is a reminder of the growth of the leisure industry. The speeding electric unit gave no warning of its approach and I had to use a 1/1,000 second shutter speed to 'stop' it. *J. F. Davies (Photomatic / Rail Archive Stephenson) / Author*

62 FOLKESTONE CENTRAL (2)

Then : 31 July 1955

'West Country' pacific No 34091 *Weymouth* from Stewarts Lane shed slows through the station with a relief Victoria to Folkestone Harbour boat train, which would have been allowed about 2 hours 20 minutes to complete the journey, including the reversal at Folkestone Junction station for the short section down to the harbour. By contrast a typical journey time from Charing Cross to Folkestone Central is now 1 hour 30 minutes. No 34091 entered traffic in September 1949 and was withdrawn in September 1964.

Now : 22 January 1996

The signalbox with its mechanical lever equipment has now been removed and the platform extended at the time of electrification. However, due to the decline in the boat train and freight traffic, the reduction in the number of trains using this route does not justify the retention of the two centre roads in the station which are rusty and unused. In the far background to the right of the picture the Channel Tunnel terminal can just be seen below the chalk escarpment.
J. F. Davies (Photomatic/Rail Archive Stephenson)/ Author

64 WESTENHANGER

Then : 1954

A general view of the station, which was opened in 1844, looking towards Ashford. Just to the east of this point the line is on a continuous descent to Dover. At the time the picture was taken the station was manned, and handled freight traffic as the sidings show. In the background is the station for Folkestone racecourse, with bay and main line platforms.

63 SHORNCLIFFE/ FOLKESTONE WEST

Then : 1949
No 34031 *Torrington* was built in June 1946 and allocated to the Eastern Section. Although in this picture the locomotive is carrying its British Railways number, the livery includes three yellow stripes retained from recent Southern Railway ownership. The train is Victoria to Dover Marine boat train composed of Continental boat train 'Matchboard' stock.

Now : 22 January 1996
The station (now renamed Folkestone West) and its surroundings, look severe and bare compared to the 1949 picture. The centre roads have been removed, the signalbox demolished and the up platform straightened out. Note though that the railings with the distinctive round top posts survive. The works on the right hand side has been removed but the house in front of it remains, fitted with modern windows. The 13.30 train from Charing Cross to Dover Priory is entering the station composed of two 4-VEP units.
A. C. Cawston (Rail Archive Stephenson)/Author

64 WESTENHANGER

Now : 22 January 1996
The present day scene shows the station building surviving, though boarded up — surely with sound proofing it has the potential to be an attractive residence? The sidings and racecourse platforms have been removed but the remains of the latter can still be seen adjacent to the concrete footbridge. New racecourse buildings have made their appearance to the left of the station, and the presence of cars in the forecourt shows that there is a modest amount of regular commuter traffic using the limited number of trains that call here in the morning and evening peak periods. *R. C. Riley/Author*

65 ASHFORD WORKS

Then : 1959

A general view of Ashford Works erecting shop showing Maunsell 2-6-0s under repair, including, in the foreground, a 'U1' class locomotive — note the CND logo on one of its buffers! On the left of the picture amidst the general clutter, so typical of locomotive works of the day, is a part from 'U' class No 31638 if the chalked identification is to be believed. This locomotive is now undergoing restoration on the Bluebell Railway in East Sussex.

Ashford Works

The old gatehouse and clocktower at the entrance to the works. *Author*

Now : 23 January 1996

A view is taken further back up the old erecting shop looking in the same direction as the previous picture. This is now the On-Track and Heavy Repair Workshop owned by Southern Track Renewals Co Ltd which operates a number of plant, track pre-assembly and welding depots around the south of England. In the foreground of the picture, Plasser general purpose 12 tonne crane No DRP 81522 from the Colchester area is receiving a bogie and major component change. Behind this, Plasser track relaying machine DRP 78224 is receiving a yearly maintenance, and Plasser Tramm No DR 98217 is being de-commissioned as a leaf clearing machine following the leaf fall season, and having a new set of wheels fitted.

Author/Author(Courtesy Southern Track Renewals Co Ltd)

66 ASHFORD (1)

Then : early 1950s

The down side of the old Ashford station sees Brighton built Fairburn 2-6-4T No 42078 after arrival with a train from Maidstone East composed of a BR Mk1 set and a Maunsell third coach. These locomotives replaced some of the old pre-Grouping designs on local passenger services before moving on to the London Midland Region with the arrival of the BR Standard 2-6-2Ts and 2-6-4Ts.

Now : 12 February 1996

The down side of the new International station with the 09.10 Eurostar service from Paris to Waterloo passing on the up through road. The station has been completely rebuilt, the rounded style of architecture on the upper level above platform 3 being reminiscent of prewar Southern Railway designs. *J. H. Aston/Author*

67 ASHFORD (2)

Then : 12 September 1954

The Railway Correspondence & Travel Society ran a memorable special train, the Invicta around Kent. It was hauled for the last section of its journey from Ashford to Blackfriars by two veteran Wainwright 4-4-0s, 'E' class No 31166 piloting 'D' class No 31737, the latter locomotive now part of the National Collection at York. Here these two lovely engines are leaving Ashford for the journey up to the Capital.

Now : 12 February 1996

The scene from this footbridge to the west of the station has been totally transformed. In the intervening years since 1954, Ashford has expanded considerably, and gone is the rural atmosphere of a small market town evident in the previous picture. Instead of fields, warehouses now overlook the line where a Eurostar service is accelerating away from the recently opened International station. The train is the 09.41 to Waterloo (08.27 from Brussels). *J. Head/Author*

69 MINSTER

Then : c1960

Minster station is located on the line from Ashford to Margate via Canterbury West opened in 1846. Shortly afterwards it became a junction when the branch to Deal was opened. This picture is taken looking towards Canterbury and shows a train for Ramsgate and Margate in the platform.

68 WYE

Then : 13 March 1955

On the line from Canterbury West opened in 1846, Wye is an attractive station situated on the northeast edge of the village and close by the Great Stour river. On a bright afternoon, No 42097, one of the Fairburn 2-6-4Ts allocated to the Southern Region in the early 1950s, brings the 2.10pm train from Margate to Ashford into the station. The train consists of a parcels van and a carmine and cream painted Maunsell three-coach set.

Now : 22 January 1996

Although the gas lights on their barley sugar posts have gone, the semaphore signalling and signalbox remain. A new and rather intrusive addition to the platform equipment is the large digital clock, many of which have been installed at stations on the Network. With numerous stations unmanned for maybe half of the day, and often lightly used by passengers outside the peak periods, the only sound to keep the traveller company is frequently the 'tok tok' of the clock as the seconds pass by. Unit No 1517 is speeding through the station with the 11.20 train from Ashford to Margate. *J. Head/Author*

69 MINSTER

Now : 21 January 1996

To be in the same position would have meant crossing electrified lines, so I have had to stand on the Canterbury-bound platform for this picture. The lines in the bay on the left have been removed, a new footbridge installed, and the substantial station buildings replaced by a simple booking office which can be seen on the far right of the picture. *D. Lawrence/Author*

70 VICTORIA (1)

Then : 14 June 1959

Victoria, opened between 1860 and 1862, is two stations in one, serving both the ex-LBSCR (London Brighton & South Coast Railway) and ex-LCDR (London Chatham & Dover Railway) lines. This is the LCDR side providing Kent coast and Continental services. 'King Arthur' class 4-6-0 No 30805 *Sir Constantine* is framed by the fine arched roof after arrival with a train from Ramsgate. This was the last day of steam on the Victoria to Kent coast lines before full electric services were brought into operation.

Now : 26 February 1996

Apart from the construction of new office accommodation, not a great deal has changed over the years, though the buffer stops have been moved forward. A train from Orpington is arriving at the platform. *Colin Hogg/Author*

71 VICTORIA (2)

Then : May 1953

In 1953 all the Bulleid pacifics were stopped to have their axles examined following an accident involving a 'Merchant Navy' locomotive at Crewkerne on 24 April. To help fill the temporary motive power shortage, some 'B1' class 4-6-0s from the Eastern Region were drafted in. One of these locomotives, No 61015 from York (50A) shed, is waiting to leave the station with a train for Ramsgate. On the left one of the solid 'King Arthur' 4-6-0s, No 30771 *Sir Sagramore*, is pulling out with another train for Ramsgate.

Now : 26 February 1996

The scene from this point is now very different. The 'Brighton' (LBSCR) side on the left of the picture has been completely rebuilt with a raft above the platforms where shops and other facilities are located (see page 94). The 11.35 train for Dover Priory is leaving the LCDR station, whose twin arches are almost lost in the background. *Colin Hogg/Author*

72 WANDSWORTH ROAD

Then : 23 May 1959

After crossing the river Thames on Grosvenor bridge, the LCDR line turns to a southeasterly direction. Working a short parcels train from the London Midland Region to Croydon, Fowler condensing 2-6-2T No 40028 passes the station which is served by trains on Victoria to London Bridge line. This was the first route electrified by the LBSCR.

Now : 26 February 1996

Not a great deal has changed, though Battersea power station, now largely hidden by the trees, is disused. Wandsworth Road offers a superb vantage point to watch the Eurostar services which join the route to the north of the station via a new flyover from the Waterloo line. The train in this picture is the 14.48 service to Maidstone East.
Colin Hogg/Author

73 CLAPHAM

Then : 30 May 1959
Within half a mile of Wandsworth Road, Clapham is a very similar station. 'C' class 0-6-0 No 31584 is working empty stock from Victoria with a smart Bulleid set behind the engine.

Now : 26 February 1996
The track layout has been altered with the removal of the centre line. An electric unit is passing with a service from Victoria to Dover.
Colin Hogg/Author

74 BRIXTON

Then : 5 October 1957

The old, if elegant, way of travelling to the Continent is depicted in this picture of the down 'Golden Arrow' passing the station in charge of 'Britannia' pacific No 70004 *William Shakespeare*, beautifully prepared by Stewarts Lane shed. The train left Victoria for Dover at 11am, the connecting service from Calais Maritime arriving at Paris Nord just before 6pm.

Now : 26 February 1996

Despite the visual appeal of the steam hauled 'Golden Arrow', the sleek lines of the new Eurostar trains, and the roar from their traction motors when on the move, are rather impressive. This is the 14.23 service from Waterloo to Paris Nord where it is due to arrive at 18.26, a considerable saving on the time taken by the 'Golden Arrow'. If by some magic the old train could be recreated, which one would you choose to travel on? *J. Head/Author*

Inset

One of two sculptures 'Platforms Piece' by Kevin Atherton at Brixton. *Author*

75 BECKENHAM JUNCTION

Then : June 1954

On summer weekends in the 1950s before widespread car ownership, an incredible procession of trains left Victoria for the Kent coast, mainly to Margate and Ramsgate. Departures at the peak times on Saturdays were every five to 15 minutes worked by every suitable engine that could be pressed into service. Among the elderly types that were still in front line use were the 'D1' and 'E1' 4-4-0s rebuilt by Maunsell from the original Wainwright designs. Here is 'D1' No 31743 getting into its stride with a Sunday excursion from Herne Hill to Ramsgate.

Now : 26 February 1996

In marked contrast to the old 4-4-0 roaring through the station, the 12.27 Eurostar service from Waterloo to Brussels is sweeping effortlessly past. The elegant semaphores have been replaced by colour light signals and the signalbox has gone. The bay platform on the left of the picture is used by trains on the line to Victoria via Crystal Palace. *S. C. Creer/Author*

76 PECKHAM RYE

Then : 8 September 1956
Despite the simple nature of its platforms, the station building here is an impressive one situated between the Catford loop and South London lines. When this picture was taken the Catford loop platforms were still constructed of wood which could be very slippery in wet weather. 'E1' class 4-4-0 No 31019, a regular performer on Kent coast expresses at this time, is passing the station with the 11.50am train from Victoria to Ramsgate.

Now : 26 February 1996
The modern platforms are much narrower than their 1950s counterparts and the picturesque old style SR lighting has been replaced by a more efficient but unattractive design. A Class 465 unit is arriving with a train for Sevenoaks.
Colin Hogg/Author

77 BECKENHAM HILL

Then : 3 June 1961

Situated on the Catford loop line, Beckenham Hill serves a number of nearby large housing estates. Southern Region Crompton (later Class 33) diesel-electric locomotive No D6545, smartly turned out in Brunswick green livery, is passing the station with the 1.30pm boat train from Victoria to Folkestone Harbour.

Now : 26 February 1996

Because the growth of vegetation in the brickwork of the bridge obscures the view from the earlier position, I have had to move to the right slightly. The station is much the same as before, though the cover over the footbridge has been removed. A train for Dover via Faversham is passing. *J. Scrace/Author*

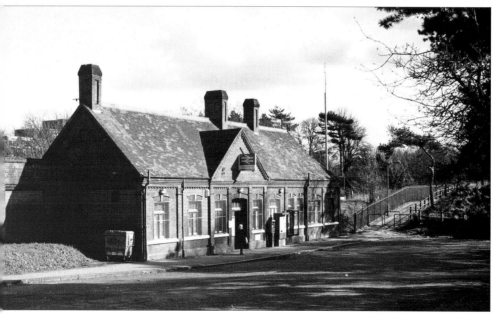

The pleasant brick built cottage style station building. *Author*

78 RAVENSBOURNE

Then : 19 May 1961

The next station on from Beckenham Hill, Ravensbourn is set in a quiet wooded valley. A rebuilt 'Battle of Britain' pacific No 34088 *213 Squadron* is passing the station with the 2.30pm train boat train from Victoria to Dover. The dirty locomotive is far removed from the generally good turn-out of boat train engines in the 1950s.

Now : 22 February 1996

On this dank winter afternoon I am the only person on the station to see the 16.00 train from Victoria to Rochester passing through.
J. Scrace/Author

79 SHORTLANDS

Then : 14 June 1958

At Shortlands Junction on the London side of the station, which can be seen in the background, the Catford loop joins the LCDR main line from Victoria via Beckenham Junction. On this hot summer afternoon, 'Schools' class No 30913 *Christ's Hospital* has come off the Catford loop line and is passing the water pumping station with a train for the Kent coast.

Now : 22 February 1996

In common with so many locations in the area, not a great deal has changed over the 38 years or so since the last picture was taken. The pump house is still there and the station is almost unchanged. The train is the 14.35 from Victoria to Dover Priory. *Colin Hogg/Author*

80 BROMLEY SOUTH

Then : 18 May 1959
Bromley South station, opened in 1858 and situated almost 11 miles from Victoria, was the first principal stopping place for some expresses to and from the Kent coast in the days of steam. However unrebuilt Bulleid pacific No 34077 *603 Squadron* is not making such a stop with the 10.30am Victoria to Dover Marine boat train.

Now : 22 February 1996
The reconstruction of the station, which was underway in the last picture, has now long been completed. The platform numbers have been altered and the direction of running changed so that London-bound trains now leave from platforms 1 and 3. A train for Orpington waits to leave from platform 2.
Colin Hogg/Author

81 ST MARY CRAY

Then : undated but c1954
The original station was opened in 1860, but this view shows the clean and functional rebuilt station. A 4-SUB unit waits in the platform with a train for Victoria.

Now : 22 February 1996
Unfortunately the station has not worn well and looked at its worst on this cheerless cold winter afternoon. The keen northeast wind blew unchecked through the broken windows on the walkway leading to the adjacent housing estates. A service from Dover to Victoria is speeding through the station.
Ian Allan Library/Author

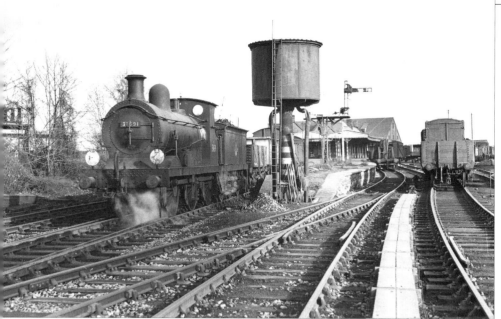

82 GRAVESEND WEST

Then : 31 January 1959

The line to Gravesend West opened in 1886, closed to passengers in 1953 and to freight in 1968. 'C' class 0-6-0 No 31691 from Hither Green shed shunting at the station before returning to the main line at Fawkham Junction.

Now : 12 February 1996

Little now remains of the old station and the site is occupied by a large car park and shops. However, the course of the short stretch of line to the pier, used at one time by Batavier line ships, is still visible. *Colin Hogg/Author*

The remains of the pier at Gravesend West. *Author*

83 GRAVESEND CENTRAL

Then : 12 July 1959

The station was the starting point for trains over the branch to Allhallows on Sea which closed to passengers in December 1961. Passenger trains were usually worked by push and pull fitted 'H' class 0-4-4Ts. One of these locomotives, No 31322, is coming into the station with a two-coach LSWR set, prior to departure on the 12.32pm service to Allhallows.

Now : 12 February 1996

A car park has replaced the old goods yard, otherwise much is the same. A Class 465 unit is arriving with a service from Charing Cross. *Colin Hogg/Author*

The nicely restored frontage on the up side of the station. *Author*

84 ALLHALLOWS ON SEA

Then : 12 July 1959

After a run of almost 15 miles from Gravesend, Allhallows was reached. Parts of the Isle of Grain, through which the line runs, are surprisingly picturesque, especially in the spring, but such qualities do not extend to Allhallows. The Southern Railway had hoped Allhallows might develop as a major holiday destination, but this was not to be. Two trains hauled by 'H' class Nos 31322 and 31164 wait to leave the windswept marshes for Gravesend.

Now : 12 February 1996

Nothing remains of the station, though much of the route from Gravesend survives to serve the large oil terminal at Grain. Chalets have been erected on the site once occupied by the station, and some of these can be seen behind the trees on the right of the picture. *Colin Hogg/Author*

The chalet site produced something of a surprise in that the old loco watering tank still survives, but whether it is used as a reservoir is not known. *Author*

85 SOLE STREET

Then : July 1958

Sole Street is a name which most older enthusiasts will remember, for it was here on summer Saturdays, that heavy holiday trains struggled up the five-mile long 1 in 100 bank from Rochester. A 'King Arthur' 4-6-0 on such a train is about to breast the summit as it passes the station with a train from Ramsgate.

Now : 12 February 1996

Apart from new lighting and the removal of advertisement boards, the station is remarkably the same. I almost hoped to see a 'E1' 4-4-0 coming roaring under the bridge, but instead had to be content with a train from Dover which is making light work of the gradient.
Both Author

86 CHATHAM

Then : 13 June 1959
The station occupies a rather cramped site between two tunnels, Fort Pitt and Chatham. This picture shows the 1.26pm train from Victoria to Ramsgate which is in charge of 'N' class No 31811. The small driving wheels of this class made them well suited for handling heavy summer Saturday trains on the steeply graded section from London.

Now : 12 February 1996
The station looks well cared for, and decorative ironwork has been installed on the apex of the roof. Electric unit No 1519 is working a Ramsgate service. *J. J. Smith/Author*

87 GILLINGHAM (KENT)

Then : 1959
'C' class 0-6-0 No 31256 is leaving the station with a local train for Sittingbourne made up of a three-coach BR Mark1 set. Gillingham tunnel, one of the numerous tunnels on the line from Rochester, precedes the approach to the station.

Now : 12 February 1996
The old buildings on the down side of the station have been demolished to be replaced by railway offices and mess-rooms. The 15.13 service to Ramsgate is leaving the platform. *Colin Hogg/Author*

88 SITTINGBOURNE

Then : Summer 1958
Preparations are in hand for the first phase of the Kent Coast Electrification scheme which took in the lines to Faversham, Ramsgate and Dover via Canterbury East. This is a summer Saturday and motive power resources will be stretched to the limit. A 'King Arthur' class 4-6-0, No 30769 *Sir Balan*, is on the 'Kentish Belle' all-Pullman train, rather than the usual Bulleid pacific. In the bay platform Ivatt 2-6-2T No 41308 waits to leave with a train to Sheerness.

Now : 23 January 1996
The line to Sheerness branches off the main line to the west of the station, the destination of this electric unit working the shuttle service to the Thames-side town. *Both Author*

89 QUEENBOROUGH (1)

Then : 1958
The 'C' class 0-6-0s, though primarily freight engines, were often used on excursions on summer Sundays. No 31298 is working such a train which is entering the station bound for Sheerness. Queenborough was the junction for the Isle of Sheppey Light Railway which ran over the marshes to Leysdown. The line closed in 1950.

Now : 23 January 1996
Although it is not long after three, the light is rapidly fading on this gloomy winter afternoon. The 15.07 train from Sittingbourne is entering the largely unaltered station to pick up a surprising number of people for the short run to Sheerness. *Both Author*

The exterior of the 1860-built station. *Author*

90 QUEENBOROUGH (2)

Then : 30 July 1949
'R1' class 0-4-4Ts were the usual motive power for the trains to Leysdown during the line's last years of operation. No 1709 has arrived in the bay platform at the station with a train from Leysdown which is made up of an articulated set and a van.

Now : 23 January 1996
The view looking towards Sheerness with the site of the one time Isle of Sheppey line bay platform on the right. *D. W. Winkworth/Author*

91 SHEERNESS EAST

Then : 21 October 1950
This was the first station on the branch to Leysdown and is seen only a few weeks before closure on 4 December 1950. The picture is taken looking towards Queenborough — it is interesting to note that although the starting signal at the end of the station platform is 'off', the level crossing gates are closed!

Now : 23 January 1996
Remarkably nearly half a century on, the platform facing can still clearly be seen among the rubble in the derelict yard.
J. J. Smith/Author

93 TEYNHAM

Then : Easter Monday 1959
Between Sittingbourne and Faversham, the station is situated amid the orchards which abound in this part of Kent. A few local people are waiting to board the train from Victoria, hauled by a 'Schools' class 4-4-0, which is drawing to a halt in the station.

92 SHEERNESS

Then : 1958
At the end of the eight-mile long branch from Sittingbourne, 'H' class 0-4-4T No 31512 is waiting to return to the main line. Standing in the centre road are two coaches, possibly for strengthening trains at busy times.

Now : 23 January 1996
The scene today is almost the same, and even the centre road has been retained. An icy northeast wind was blowing across the Thames Estuary on this winter afternoon, so the passengers for Sittingbourne were thankful to retreat into the warmth of the 15.56 train to Sittingbourne which is about to leave.
Colin Hogg/Author

93 TEYNHAM

Now : 22 January 1996
A new waiting shelter has been constructed on the down platform, otherwise little has changed. The 13.31 train to Ramsgate, which is entering the station, is running about 10 minutes late due to operational problems nearer London.
Both Author

The pleasant traditional level crossing at Teynham station giving access to the station houses and the marshes. *Author*

94 FAVERSHAM (1)

Then : 18 May 1959
Faversham is the junction for the line to Dover via Canterbury East. Three-cylinder 'U1' class 2-6-0 No 31907 is arriving at the station with the 3.28pm train from Dover to Victoria. The locomotive shed (73E) is to the right of centre in the picture, and is situated in the fork between the Dover and Ramsgate lines. About 30 locomotives were allocated to this shed in the 1950s and were employed on local passenger and freight turns.

Now : 22 January 1996
Gone is much of the bustle of earlier years though the station is still an important junction. A stopping train from Ramsgate is arriving and will connect with a train from Dover Priory. Although disused, the locomotive shed is still standing, one of the few such buildings to survive. *Colin Hogg/Author*

95 FAVERSHAM (2)

Then : 2 June 1959

This picture is taken from the long footbridge which spans the Dover and Ramsgate lines to the east of the station. It shows the 9.35am Victoria to Ramsgate train which is in charge of 'Schools' class No 30909 *St Paul's*. The shed is to the left of the picture, whilst on the other side of the line, a Maunsell 2-6-0 is preparing to leave the goods yard with an up freight train.

Now : 22 January 1996

A stopping train for Ramsgate is leaving the station. To the left of the picture the rails in the one-time shed yard have been lifted. The footbridge gives an excellent view of the derelict shed buildings. *Antony Linaker/Author*

96 WHITSTABLE

Then : undated but probably the early summer of 1959

Once the pride of Stewarts Lane shed, 'King Arthur' No 30768 *Sir Balin* leaves the station with a down express for Ramsgate. The platforms have been extended in connection with electrification. To the east of the station the Canterbury & Whitstable Railway, closed completely in 1953, crossed the main line.

Now : 22 January 1996

The bridge from which the last picture was taken has been demolished, so I could not secure a direct comparison. There is very little variety in the trains along this line. Typical of the service is this stopping train for Ramsgate which is passing the platform extension shown in the 'Then' photograph.
P. Ransome-Wallis/Author

97 WESTGATE-ON-SEA

Then : 11 April 1959

The station, which was opened in 1871, is situated on the western outskirts of Margate. Standard Class 5 No 73086 is calling at the station some 23 minutes after leaving Ramsgate with this train to Victoria.

Now : 21 January 1996

There is almost more illumination from the lights on the station platform than from the sky to enable me to photograph the arrival of the 15.38 service to Victoria. The station buildings still survive, and the other Victorian and Edwardian properties in the vicinity give the whole area a feeling of times past. *D. W. Winkworth/Author*

98 MARGATE (1)

Then : 9 May 1959
A view of Margate from the western end of the yard showing 'King Arthur' No 30806 *Sir Galleron* leaving the station with the 1.55pm Ramsgate to Victoria train.

Now : 21 January 1996
The station canopies have been cut back and the sidings removed, whilst in the background a tower block dominates the skyline — otherwise not a great deal has changed. *D. W. Winkworth/Author*

99 MARGATE (2)

Then : March 1959

As noted under the entry for Beckenham Junction (page 64), traffic to the Kent coast was intensive at holiday times. Some flavour of the busy service is given in this picture of 'L' class No 31768 and 'L1' class No 31758, standing in the platforms after arrival from Faversham. The train reporting number carried by the 'L1' suggests a augmented service was in operation, so the picture may have been taken during the Easter holiday.

Now : 21 January 1996

The dense service of holiday trains has gone, the victim of widespread car ownership and changing leisure habits. However, on this cold and quiet Sunday afternoon the station itself looks little altered. *Ian Allan Library/Author*

The new station was built in the late 1920s on the site of the old Margate West. The frontage was designed on an heroic scale, and even today is very impressive. *Author*

100 RAMSGATE

Then : 6 April 1953
Trains leave Ramsgate in either direction for London, via Margate on the LCDR route, southwestwards on the former SER lines to Deal and Dover, or through Minster and Ashford. No 30915 *Brighton* is leaving the station in the Dover direction. The side wall of the shed (74A) can be seen on the left of the picture. It had an allocation of some 50 locomotives in the 1950s, including a number of Bulleid light pacifics.

Now : 21 January 1996
This picture gives a good idea of the importance of Ramsgate as a major electric rolling stock depot. This building now stands on the area once occupied by the old steam shed. A Class 411 unit is leaving the station bound for the carriage sidings. *R. C. Riley/Author*

101 CANTERBURY EAST

Then : 20 June 1954
The station was opened in 1860. At the time this picture was taken it still had its attractive all-over roof. Ivatt 2-6-2T No 41308 is leaving the station with the 2pm train from Faversham to Dover Priory. In contrast to the busy line to Ramsgate, the Dover line had a very sparse service on summer Saturdays in the early 1950s. For example there was a two-hour gap in both directions in mid-afternoon.

Now : 23 January 1996
Unfortunately the gates to the yard on the left of the picture were locked so I was unable to repeat the 1954 picture exactly. However, this view shows that the overall roof has gone, but the striking tall signalbox remains to control the semaphore signals. *N. W. Sprinks/Author*

103 SHEPHERDS WELL (EAST KENT RAILWAY) (1)

Then : 15 March 1946
The East Kent Light Railway remained independent until 1948, but passenger services were withdrawn on 30 October of that year. Not long after the war, EKR No 2, an 'O1' class 0-6-0, waits to leave the station with the 5pm mixed train to Canterbury Road and Wingham.

102 SHEPHERDS WELL

Then : August 1960
Shepherds Well was the junction for the East Kent Light Railway which was engineered by Colonel Stephens. In its last years the line served Tilmanstone colliery and was worked by 'O1' class 0-6-0s from Dover shed. No 31065 is standing in the exchange sidings by the main line as 'N' class 2-6-0 No 31811 approaches with a train for Dover.

Now : 21 January 1996
The East Kent Railway closed completely in the mid 1980s but some traces of the exchange sidings remain. A Sunday morning train for Dover is approaching the station.
G. R. Siviour/Author

103 SHEPHERDS WELL (EAST KENT RAILWAY) (1)

Now : 21 January 1996
The new East Kent Light Railway has recently reopened the railway as far as Eythorne and operates the service using ex-BR diesel multiple-units. One of these units is waiting to leave on the 11.00 service. Situated towards the rear of the station, a new booking office has been modelled on the original EKR design.
D. W. Winkworth/Author

104 SHEPHERDS WELL (EAST KENT RAILWAY) (2)

Then : 9 September 1948
Shortly before the cessation of passenger services, the 5pm mixed train waits to leave the station. The train is being worked by EKR No 6, the one-time SR 'O' class 0-6-0 No 372. This locomotive, which was sold to the EKR in 1923, was fitted with an 'O1' class boiler at Ashford in 1945.

Now : 21 January 1996
The same view looking towards Eythorn showing the new booking office and some of the railway's stock. *J. J. Smith/Author*

106 MAIDSTONE EAST

Then : 1958
The station dates from 1874 as part of the LCDR route to Ashford opened in 1884. In this picture a BR Standard Class 2 2-6-2T is waiting to leave with a train for Ashford which will call at all stations.

105 EYTHORNE

Then : 23 November 1957

Just over a mile from Shepherds Well the line arrives at Eythorne station which is situated between the villages of Eythorne and Lower Eythorne. This is the view looking north towards Tilmanstone.

Now : 21 January 1996

Eythorne is the present limit of operation on the EKR. A new station has been constructed on the site of the old one.
D. W. Winkworth/Author

106 MAIDSTONE EAST

Now : 12 February 1996

Though electric signals have been installed the station is still very much the same. The evening rush is getting under way with the arrival of the 15.55 semi-fast train to Ashford. *Both Author*

107 BEARSTED

Then : 1958
Standard Class 2 2-6-2T No 84024 is arriving at the station with a stopping service for Ashford. A batch of these locomotives, Nos 84020 to 84029, were built at Darlington in 1957 for use on the Southern Region. They were fitted with push and pull gear but it was later removed.

Now : 12 February 1996
A new footbridge has been erected at the station which frames a Class 423/1 unit arriving with a stopping train for Ashford. Like Hollingbourne, the station is well situated for the nearby Leeds Castle. There is a special bus service to the castle for tourists using the station. *Both Author*

108 CHARING

Then : undated

The station is situated on the southwestern outskirts of the village. An ex-LMS 2-6-4T is arriving with a stopping train from Maidstone East to Ashford.

Now : 23 January 1996

As at Bearsted, a new concrete footbridge has been erected which hides the up platform shelter. The station looks smart and well maintained — note the safety lines on both platforms. *R. C. Riley/Author*

109 LONDON BRIDGE

Then : 14 August 1960

The high arched roof of the 'Brighton' terminus at London Bridge, which serves lines to East Croydon and the south coast, makes for a more spacious and imposing station than the functional one for the South Eastern routes to the left of this picture. In this view, 'C' class No 31293 is passing the large signalbox to arrive at the Brighton station with the 6.8pm empty stock train from New Cross Gate.

Now : 26 January 1996

Modern signalling, track and platform changes can be seen in this present day picture. Over on the South Eastern side, a Class 466 unit is approaching the station. On one of the far tracks, a two car de-icing train, made up from a BR 1960s built suburban set, provides a focus of interest. *Colin Hogg/Author*

110 NEW CROSS GATE

Then : 15 August 1955

New Cross Gate is at the foot of a 1 in 100 gradient up to Forest Hill which could tax the locomotives of heavy freight trains. In this picture an ex-LBSCR 'E6' 0-6-2T No 32412 is providing rear end assistance for the locomotive hauling the 2.15pm freight to Norwood Junction. The shed at New Cross Gate closed after the World War 2 and its final role was for the storage of withdrawn or surplus locomotives, including, in 1951, two partially completed members of the 'Leader' class.

Now : 29 February 1996

Apart from the removal of some of the buildings on the centre platforms, the station remains very much the same. The shed, which was to the right of the picture, has long been demolished and the site is now occupied by a supermarket. A Thameslink train for Bedford is passing the station. *P. Howland/Author*

111 HONOR OAK PARK

Then : 20 June 1957

The next station out from New Cross Gate, Honor Oak Park, was a good vantage point to watch southbound steam-hauled trains climbing the 1 in 100 gradient. On this wet and thundery day, 'U1' class No 31910 is in charge of the 12.20pm Saturdays only train from London Bridge to Tunbridge Wells West. At this time many firms still worked a five and a half day week, so this train would have been conveying office workers home at the start of their weekend.

Now : 29 February 1996

Today the station is rather characterless and depressing, though essentially unchanged. A train from Norwood Junction and East Croydon is arriving at the down platform. *Colin Hogg/Author*

112 VICTORIA

Then : 1970

The old platform 13 at Victoria showing the 14.00 'Brighton Belle' service which is ready to receive its compliment of passengers. A supplementary fare was charged on this non-stop all-Pullman service to Brighton. By this time the '5-BEL' electric units had lost their colourful traditional Pullman livery in favour of the rather dreary British Rail corporate blue and grey. Points of interest are the platform ticket machine and the splendid ironwork of the platform gate, barrier railings and station roof.

Now : 26 January 1996

The new platform 13 at Victoria. A modern terminal for the Gatwick Express trains, incorporating a shopping mall and offices, has now been built over the Brighton line platforms. Perhaps in years to come this picture will form an interesting 'Then' view for it illustrates some features of modern living. Note for example the display and prices for the hamburgers, the credit card advertisement and the security camera. Compared with the 1970 picture, the surroundings look clean and glossy though the warning notice on the right of the destination board warns how slippery the new polished tiled floor surface can become when wet. *Both Author*

113 CLAPHAM JUNCTION (1)

Then : 1953

It has long been the custom of the Queen to travel to the Derby by train. This is her special Pullman car train to Tattenham Corner which is being worked by a superbly turned out 'Schools' locomotive, No 30915 *Brighton* from Stewarts Lane shed. It is proudly carrying the Royal Headcode, and note the white-painted embellishments including the wheel tyres.

Now : 29 February 1996

The elevated signalbox on the Western Section side of the station has been removed following its collapse in the 1960s, but the brick-built box on the 'Brighton' side remains, though out of use. After a cautious exit from Victoria through Battersea Park, Class 73 No 73202 is gathering speed through the station with a Gatwick Express.
Colin Hogg/Author

Inset

The sign that says it all at Clapham Junction.
Author

114 CLAPHAM JUNCTION (2)

Then : 3 May 1963

Clapham Junction offered the opportunity to see a variety of locomotives from other BR Regions working transfer freights. An example is this Norwood Junction to Willesden train of empty coal wagons cautiously approaching the station down the 1 in 166 gradient from Wandsworth Common. The locomotive is Willesden-based '8F' 2-8-0 No 48629.

Now : 29 February 1996

Apart from the housing in the old goods yard, the scene looks very much the same — a local train from Wandsworth Common is being overtaken by an up Gatwick Express.
Brian Stephenson/Author

115 CRYSTAL PALACE LOW LEVEL

Then : 15 October 1962

Of particular interest at Crystal Palace are the substantial station buildings opened in 1854. These provide an impressive background for 'Q' class 0-6-0 No 30538 passing through the station with empty coaching stock for East Croydon. To the rear of the train on the other side of the bridge, the line for Sydenham veers off to the left. By this time the LCD High Level station had closed, hence the blanking out of the words 'Low Level' on the nameboard on the left hand side of the picture.

Now : 15 April 1996

Some of the station buildings have been demolished, but otherwise not a great deal has changed. The a train for Norwood Junction and East Croydon is arriving at the platform. *Brian Stephenson/Author*

116 EAST CROYDON

Then : 6 March 1954

This is the view from the end of the platform looking towards London. Standard Class 4 2-6-0 No 76006 working the 12.3pm Victoria to Brighton train, is passing under the fine gantry of ex-LBSCR signals that dominates the approach to the station. Always a busy station, the electric and steam services leave here for almost every part of the old LBSCR system.

Now : 29 February 1996

Croydon in the 1990s is a major office and shopping centre and the station has been rebuilt to meet modern requirements, though the basic layout remains the same. The view from the north end of the platforms is now dominated by office buildings. A service for Tunbridge Wells via Redhill and Tonbridge is arriving at the station. *Colin Hogg/Author*

117 SOUTH CROYDON

Then : 2 June 1963

To the south of the station the line to Oxted turns off to the left. Looking in the other direction towards East Croydon a LMR Class 5 No 45434 is working a Whit Sunday Nuneaton to Brighton excursion, one of many such trains which used this line at holiday times. One of the tall new office blocks in central Croydon is under construction.

Now : 15 April 1996

The view from this footbridge has not changed a great deal over the years. Adding some variety to the procession of electric units which pass through the station, two Class 33 diesel-electric locomotives hurry south on an unknown mission. *J. Scrace/Author*

119 OXTED

Then : 1962

At the time this picture was taken, services to Ashurst and Tunbridge Wells West were provided by 'H' class 0-4-4Ts using push and pull stock. No 31522 is running through the down platform before setting back into the bay platform which can be seen on the right hand side of the picture.

118 UPPER WARLINGHAM

Then : 6 June 1962

The station is situated close to Whyteleafe on the side of a narrow chalk valley on the line to Oxted. It was favoured by railway photographers for recording the southbound evening business trains from Victoria and London Bridge. One of these trains, the 6.15pm from London Bridge to Tunbridge Wells West, is leaving the station hauled by Standard 2-6-4T No 80010.

Now : 15 April 1996

The goods yard has been converted to a car park, patronised largely by commuters who use the electrified service on the East Grinstead and Oxted line. One of these trains, the 15.24 from Victoria, is leaving the station for East Grinstead. *Colin Hogg/Author*

119 OXTED

Now : 15 April 1996

The station buildings have now been rebuilt, and the former goods yard, out of sight behind me on the up side, is the location for a new supermarket, currently in course of construction. The 16.23 train from Victoria to East Grinstead is arriving at the station at the start of the evening rush. The down bay platform, just in view on the right hand side of the picture, is still in use, and the departure point for the restricted diesel-electric train service to Edenbridge and Uckfield. Note the young man on the right carrying that indispensible accessory of modern living, the mobile phone! *Both Author*

120 HURST GREEN HALT/HURST GREEN

Then : 1957
One of the BR Standard Class 4 2-6-4Ts, No 80011 from Tunbridge Wells shed, is about to stop at the old concrete-built halt with a train for its home town. Just south of the halt the lines to Tunbridge Wells and East Grinstead separate.

Now : 15 April 1996
I could not repeat the above picture exactly without trespassing, so have taken this view with a telephoto lens from the footbridge which spans the junction of the Uckfield and East Grinstead lines. The 16.34 train from Oxted to Uckfield is passing the site of the old Halt. *Both Author*

With the growth of population in the Oxted area and associated new housing development, the halt became inadequate to cope with rising passenger numbers. This is the new station on the Oxted side of the bridge on 23 February 1996. A train for East Grinstead is entering the down platform. *Author*

121 EDENBRIDGE TOWN

Then : 1960

Edenbridge Town is the station on the LBSCR line from Oxted to Ashurst and Eridge (see also page 24 — Edenbridge). At the time this picture was taken, local services between Oxted and Tunbridge Wells West were worked mainly by ex-SECR 'H' class 0-4-4Ts such as No 31544, which is shown leaving the station with a southbound train. The goods yard is still in use for coal traffic.

Now : 23 February 1996

Following the recent accident at Cowden, a limited service of trains runs over this line between Oxted and Uckfield (see page 99 — Uckfield). On this pleasant winter afternoon, the 13.34 train from Oxted is leaving the station. This picture gives a good view of the LBSCR station cottages which were obscured by the steam in the previous picture. Similar cottages can be seen at Horsted Keynes on the Bluebell Railway. *Both Author*

The attractive and nicely maintained station building at Edenbridge Town on 23 February 1996. For those who like 'Brighton' country stations, a visit is well worthwhile. *Author*

122 ASHURST

Then : 1958

Three stations further on from Edenbridge Town is Ashurst, situated close by the infant River Medway. The platform clock shows 4.30 on this sunny afternoon as this push and pull service from Oxted to Tunbridge Wells West pauses at the station. Note the signalbox on the platform with its protecting iron railings. The locomotive is 'H' class 0-4-4T No 31177 from Tonbridge shed.

Now : 23 February 1996

The delightful station buildings have now been demolished, leaving only the minimum of facilities. Diesel-electric unit No 205025, on the 14.30 service from Uckfield, is pausing at the station to set down a lone passenger.
Both Author

123 WITHYHAM

Then : undated but likely to be the mid-1950s
Withyham station on the line from East Grinstead High Level to
Ashurst Junction closed in January 1967. The line ran through
pleasant but sparsely populated country, and closure was not
unexpected. The Brighton-built BR Standard Class 4 2-6-4Ts, such as
No 80151 working this train for East Grinstead, were regular
performers on the line in the mid-1950s

Now : 23 February 1996
The route of the line at this point is now part of the Forest Way
Country Park. The station is a private residence and, as the picture
shows, its platform survives. *Ian Allan Library/Author*

124 GROOMBRIDGE

Then : March 1962

This station, on the line from East Grinstead to Tunbridge Wells West, was opened in 1866. Standard 2-6-4T No 80088 is departing with a service from Tunbridge Wells West to Oxted. The pride that has been lavished on the station is evident from the diamond-shaped rose beds in the neatly mown lawn. Note the member of staff sweeping the platform.

Now : 13 February 1996

What remains of the station has now been converted to offices, whilst the rest of the site has been given over to housing development. Whether the new houses were supposed to encroach so near to the remaining single line to Tunbridge Wells, I do not know. A few of the occupants are certainly going to have an unrivalled view of the Spa Valley Railway trains when the Tunbridge Wells & Eridge Railway Preservation Society (TWERPS) eventually start operating a service between here and Tunbridge Wells! Their station is located on the other side of the bridge on which I am standing. *Brian Haresnape/Author*

The TWERPS station at Groombridge looking west on 13 February 1996. *Author*

125 TUNBRIDGE WELLS WEST

Then : 16 June 1963
This fine LBSCR station, with its massive clock tower, was opened in 1866. Situated on the western edge of the town, the station was linked to Tunbridge Wells Central via the line through Grove tunnel and Grove Junction where it joined the SER route from Hastings. Rebuilt Bulleid pacific No 34088 *213 Squadron* is leaving the station with a special empty stock working to New Cross Gate. The locomotive shed (75F) can be seen to the immediate left of the locomotive. This structure is still standing and used by the Tunbridge Wells & Eridge Railway Preservation Society (TWERPS).

Now : 13 January 1996
The line from Ashurst Junction to Tunbridge Wells has closed. The station site is now owned by Sainsbury, and I have had to move slightly nearer the station to take this picture because of the erection of new buildings. Happily the station has been incorporated in the fresh development, and is now a Beefeater restaurant 'The Old West Station'. The back end of the shed can be seen on the extreme left of the picture. *S. C. Nash/Author*

Detail of the clock tower and station on 13 January 1996. *Author*

126 ERIDGE

Then : 14 April 1962

Eridge was the junction for Cuckoo line trains to Heathfield and Eastbourne which branched off the Uckfield line at Redgate Mill Junction south of the station. 'N' class No 31824 has arrived with the 1.55pm train from Brighton to Victoria, and some passengers are changing into the 1.45pm train from Eastbourne to Tonbridge which is standing at the adjacent platform.

Now : 13 January 1996

The atmospheric station is now the headquarters of TWERPS (see page 105 [Tunbridge Wells West]), and some of their stock, including Class 50 diesel-electric No 50019 *Ramillies*, can be seen on the extreme left of the picture. The only trains currently using the station are those on the infrequent service from Oxted to Uckfield. The 14.30 from Uckfield is arriving but there are no passengers. *D. W. Winkworth/Author*

128 ISFIELD

Then : 1960

By 1958 there were no 'Schools' class 4-4-0s left at St Leonards shed where they had been the mainstay of services up to London (see page 43 [West St Leonards]). No 30901 *Winchester*, one of the last of the class to leave, was transferred to Brighton. Compared to the demands of the steeply graded Hastings to Tunbridge Wells line, most duties the class undertook from Brighton were far easier — this three-coach stopping train from Brighton to Victoria via Eridge and Oxted was typical. Eventually No 30901 was withdrawn from service at the end of 1962.

127 UCKFIELD

Then : 1953

This is the old station at Uckfield showing a train from Brighton to Tonbridge waiting to leave. It is pure SECR — the locomotive is No 31166, the last 'E' class 4-4-0 left in service, whilst the coaches are made up of a 'Birdcage' set. No 31166 lingered on at Tonbridge shed for a little while longer before being scrapped at Ashford where it had been built in 1907 (see also page 58).

Now : 14 January 1996

Southwards from Uckfield towards Isfield and Lewes, the line is now closed (but see the entry for Isfield). The old station has been abandoned thus allowing the removal of the level crossing and the footbridge. A new station with a single platform has been opened immediately to the north of the old level crossing, and this is served by a limited service of trains from Oxted. *Gerald Siviour/Author*

128 ISFIELD

Now : 7 January 1996

Although the Uckfield to Lewes line closed in 1969, Isfield station has become the headquarters of the Lavender Line which operates trains for a short distance northwards toward Uckfield. Work is underway to relay the yard as a train consisting of diesel multiple-coaches is propelled up the line by Hunslet tank engine *Cunarder* which was previously based on the Swanage Railway.
Gerald Siviour/Author

129 MAYFIELD

Then : 17 April 1965

Mayfield is on the line from Redgate Mill Junction south of Eridge, to Polegate. This was popularly known as the 'Cuckoo Line', losing its service in 1968. This picturesque route ran through lovely Wealden countryside, but because of the sparsely populated nature of the area, never benefited from large numbers of passengers. Some services, such as this diesel-multiple unit, worked through from Tonbridge to Eastbourne. The signalman is handing over the single line token to the driver for the next section to Heathfield.

Now : 17 March 1996

The line of the trackbed has been cut away to create a by-pass round the village centre leaving the down side station buildings high and dry at the top of the new embankment. The reference point in both pictures is the gable end of the station roof. This view is looking north, but by necessity further over to the left than the original photograph. *Andrew Muckley/Author*

131 HELLINGLY

Then : 17 April 1965

Taken on the same wet day as the Mayfield picture, unit No 1304 is returning north with a train to Tunbridge Wells West. Hellingly was notable for the short electrified line which served a nearby mental hospital, and the course of this railway can still be seen.

130 HEATHFIELD

Then : 28 September 1963

At Heathfield the line emerged out of a tunnel into the station which was centrally situated in the town. BR Standard 2-6-4T No 80094 has just arrived with a train for Eastbourne and is crossing a northbound diesel-electric service.

Now : 17 March 1996

The station area is now the Station Road industrial estate. Apart from the tunnel, nothing remains of the railway, but the houses on the skyline are good points of reference.
J. N. Faulkner/Author

131 HELLINGLY

Now : 17 March 1996

The station has survived as a private residence alongside the Cuckoo Trail which follows the trackbed of the railway. I have taken the picture from the bridge which spans the trackbed at the north end of the station in order to give a better view of the location as it is now. *Andrew Muckley/Author*

132 LINGFIELD

Then : 1958
Even on this miserable wet day the station looks attractive and well cared for. The fine station buildings date from the opening of this section in 1884. I took this picture from the very wide footbridge which linked the down and up platforms. There was a covered walkway to Lingfield racecourse from the up platform. The footbridge was moved to Sheffield Park on the Bluebell railway a few years ago where its width is ideal for handling the large numbers of visitors using the station. BR Standard Class 4 2-6-4T No 80151 is on a train for Tunbridge wells.

Now : 23 February 1996
The bay platform on the down side of the platform once used for race trains is no longer operational and, as noted above, the footbridge has been moved to Sheffield Park. A train from Victoria to East Grinstead is arriving at the down platform. *Both Author*

134 KINGSCOTE

Then : 1958
After closure of the line by British Railways in 1955, a local resident discovered that closure was in fact illegal under the original act, and could only be effected by Parliamentary authority. Whilst such authority was being obtained, British Railways was obliged to provide a token service between East Grinstead and Lewes which it did from August 1956 until final closure in 1958. Here one of the trains operated under the special service passes Kingscote where it did not stop, since this station (and Barcombe) was not specified when the line was first authorised. The train consists of one LBSCR compartment brake coach hauled by a Fairburn 2-6-4T No 42106.

133 EAST GRINSTEAD LOW LEVEL/EAST GRINSTEAD

Then : 19 September 1957

The history of the Lewes to East Grinstead line has been well documented in numerous publications in connection with the Bluebell Railway which was founded in 1959 and opened in August 1960. The original LBSCR line opened in 1882 and finally closed on 16 March 1958. Shortly before this date BR Standard 2-6-4T No 80149, built at Brighton, waits to leave the Low Level station with a train for Lewes. The High Level station served trains on the Three Bridges to Tunbridge Wells West, and trains from London via St. Margarets Junction. 'H' class 0-4-4T No 31544 is waiting to leave the High Level station with a train for Three Bridges.

Now : 7 January 1996

The High Level station has been closed and demolished whilst the original LBSCR buildings at the Low Level have been replaced by modern single-storey units. A train from Victoria is drawing to a halt in the station. Until Bluebell Railway trains reach East Grinstead, a bus to Kingscote connects with trains to and from London. The site of the Bluebell Railway's new station is to the right of the picture. *J. H. Aston/Author*

134 KINGSCOTE

Now : 21 August 1995

Kingscote station was re-opened on 23 April 1994, the latest phase in the Bluebell Railway's Northern Extension from Horsted Keynes to East Grinstead. The previous picture was taken from the signalbox which was demolished when the line was dismantled. This view is taken from the new down platform which is in course of construction. 'King Arthur' 4-6-0 No 30777 *Sir Lamiel*, which was on loan from the National Railway Museum, is arriving at the splendidly restored station with a special train.
Both Author

135 WEST HOATHLY

Then : 1958

Situated just to the north of the 731yd long Sharpthorne tunnel, the station served the villages of Sharpthorne and West Hoathly, the latter situated high on the sandstone ridge through which the tunnel runs. Standard 2-6-4T No 80145 from Brighton shed is leaving the station with one of the trains on the token service (sometimes known as the 'sulky service'), bound for Lewes.

Now : 7 January 1996

No trace now remains of the old station save for the platform facings. 'H' class 0-4-4T No 263 is coming south with a train from Kinsgcote to Horsted Keynes and Sheffield Park. *Both Author*

137 SHEFFIELD PARK

Then : 16 April 1955

There was no indication of the momentous changes that were to occur at Sheffield Park when this picture was taken shortly before first closure of the line in May 1955. Standard 2-6-4T tank No 80016 is one of batch assigned when new in late 1951 to Tunbridge Wells West shed. The locomotive is working the 12.3pm train from Victoria to Brighton which was due at Sheffield Park at 2.1pm. This was the leisurely and scenic way to travel from Victoria to Brighton, this train taking just under two and three quarter hours to complete the journey.

136 HORSTED KEYNES

Then : 7 May 1955

Horsted Keynes was the junction with the line from Haywards Heath. It was electrified in 1935 and closed on 27 October 1963. This is the view looking south with the Haywards Heath line curving out of sight to the left of the signal box. Ivatt 2-6-2T No 41317 is leaving the station with the 4.3pm train from Lewes to East Grinstead consisting of three-coach Bulleid and SECR 'Birdcage' sets.

Now : 14 February 1996

The scene almost 40 years later shows how well the Bluebell Railway has preserved the atmosphere and character of this country junction. Who would have thought that ex-LMS and GWR 2-6-2Ts could be photographed from the same position so many years apart. Illustrated here, is ex-GWR 2-6-2T No 4561, which visited the line from the West Somerset Railway for a few weeks earlier this year. The locomotive is leaving the station on a gauging run to Kingscote prior to entering normal service. *Colin Hogg/Author*

137 SHEFFIELD PARK

Now : 5 August 1995

Just over 40 years on, and Sheffield Park station is a scene of bustle and activity. The picture is taken from the footbridge which came from Lingfield (see page 110) and shows the shop on the right hand side of the picture. The occasion is the 35th Anniversary Weekend. The train, which represents the first Bluebell Railway service run on the line on 7 August 1960, is hauled by 'H' class 0-4-4T No 263 and 'P' class 0-6-0T No 323 *Bluebell*. *Colin Hogg/Author*

138 WEST CROYDON

Then : 23 October 1954
No 1805, one of the two-coach units converted from LBSCR overhead electric stock, is about to leave bay platform with a train for Wimbledon. These units had a great deal of character and were affectionately known by enthusiasts as the '2 Train' by virtue of their two coaches and the route headcode the units carried.

Now : 15 April 1995
The station has enjoyed a general sprucing up and the semaphore signals have been removed. Trains for Wimbledon still use the same bay platform where a Class 456 unit has just arrived from Wimbledon. It will return as the 13.00 departure. *Colin Hogg/Author*

140 MITCHAM

Then : 23 October 1954
One of the two-car units, No 1805, is working the 12.51pm West Croydon to Wimbledon service. At this time trains ran at least every 30 minutes including Sundays.

139 MITCHAM JUNCTION

Then : December 1959

The Wimbledon to West Croydon line crosses the Balham to Hackbridge and Sutton line at Mitcham Junction. The former route, opened in 1855, follows the course of the old horse worked Surrey Iron Railway. Unusually for an electrified line in an urban area, it is single track for most of the way. On the 'main line' ex-LBSCR 'E4' class 0-6-2T No 32470 from Horsham (75D) shed is standing in the down platform with a Christmas parcels train from Bricklayers Arms to Dorking North. During the pre-Christmas rush a variety of old engines were pressed into service on these interesting extra trains.

Now : 17 January 1996

Very little has changed at the station where two-car electric unit No 456015 is about to leave with the 13.30 service to West Croydon. Wimbledon to West Croydon line trains run on Mondays to Saturdays only at approximately 45-50 minute intervals. *Gerald Siviour/Author*

140 MITCHAM

Now : 17 January 1996

I was totally unprepared for the shock I felt on first seeing the station as it is now. Everything that could be broken had been and there was graffiti and litter everywhere. If any picture in this book typifies the malaise of modern society and the effect of removing staff from stations in urban areas, this must be it. Unit No 465015 is calling at the station with the 13.00 service from West Croydon to Wimbledon. There are plans to convert this line to a tramway system similar to the one in Manchester. However, this may be delayed due to funding difficulties. *J. J. Smith/Author*

141 WALLINGTON

Then : 20 June 1954

On this hot summer morning, 'N' class 2-6-0 No 31409 is in charge of the Garex (guaranteed excursion) train from Carshalton to Margate. The long train (which looks as if it might contain a Pullman coach in the middle of the formation) has just passed a London-bound electric unit which is waiting for the excursion to overtake. Beautiful mature elm trees border the coal yard which contains a fine horse drawn wagon labelled on the side: 'COAL.COKE.BOILER FUEL'.

Now : 17 January 1996

By comparison, the present image looks stark and unattractive. In addition to the track rationalisation that has taken place, the coal yard has been replaced by a cramped car park for the office development by the station. The trees to the rear of the car park have suffered serious damage over the years and may even be dead. Unit No 319018 is approaching the station with a train from Sutton to London Bridge. *Colin Hogg/Author*

143 HOLMWOOD

Then : 27 June 1969

Holmwood is situated on the line from Dorking to Horsham. It was opened in 1867 as part of the LBSCR mid-Sussex route from London to Littlehampton, Bognor and Portsmouth. The station is some distance from the villages of North and South Holmwood. A '4-SUB' unit No 4731 is entering the station with the 17.02 train from Waterloo to Horsham. Note the booking office over the line.

142 CHEAM

Then : c1960
When this picture was taken, the up and down through roads were still in use. BR Standard tank No 80088 is working a Christmas parcels train towards Epsom and Dorking. Behind the engine is a smart ex-LNER Gresley parcels van followed by two smaller ex-SR vans. No 80088 was one of a batch of locomotives built at Brighton during 1954-55. The bridge in the background carries the A217 road over the railway.

Now : 17 January 1996
For once the weather has been kind to give a repeat of the sunny conditions in the 1960 picture. Reduced traffic levels have obviated the need for the centre roads which have been removed. The old SR station lights have gone and so have the telegraph posts and wires which were so much part of the earlier railway scene. A train from Sutton to Epsom is entering the station. *Gerald Siviour/Author*

143 HOLMWOOD

Now : 10 January 1996
Nowadays the station has an hourly service in each direction on weekdays in the off-peak period. There is also an hourly non-stop service between Dorking and Horsham, such as the 11.54am train from Dorking which is seen passing the station. Though most of the buildings have been demolished, the pleasant shelter on the up platform has survived. So too have the semaphore signals, though this section is normally switched out. *J. Scrace/Author*

144 PURLEY

Then : 17 April 1954

When this picture was taken the fast lines were nearest the camera. 'Schools' 4-4-0 No 30919 *Harrow* makes an fine sight accelerating through the station with the heavy 10.5am Victoria to Newhaven Harbour boat train which will connect with the ship for Dieppe. Note the fine LBSCR signal and box to the left of the engine.

Now : 15 April 1996

Almost exactly 42 years later the scene at Purley is very different. The fast lines have been moved to the far side, where one of the frequent Gatwick Express trains is heading south on the down line. The signalbox has gone and the platforms have been extended, but the link with the past is the house on the right hand side of the picture. The old goods yard is now a busy aggregates depot served by rail.
Colin Hogg/Author

The imposing frontage of the station at Purley on 15 April 1996. *Author*

145 COULSDON NORTH

Then : 28 July 1956

Working one of the many steam-hauled trains that used the Brighton main line, 'N' class 2-6-0 No 31408 is passing the station with a Maidenhead to Eastbourne excursion. The engine is steaming freely and will shortly reach the end of the long climb out of London at Star Lane box. The train is taking the Quarry line opened by the LBSCR in 1899 to avoid the congested junction at Redhill, which it shared with the SER. In the left hand background are the platforms and signalbox of Smitham station on the Tattenham Corner branch.

Now : 15 April 1996

Coulsdon North closed in 1983 and traffic was transferred to the adjacent Smitham station. A Gatwick Express is speeding south past the remains of the station platforms.
Colin Hogg/Author

146 REDHILL

Then : 17 October 1959

Trains on the old SER route from Tonbridge to Reading had to reverse at Redhill. This train from Ramsgate to Birkenhead is coming off the line from Tonbridge to cross over the Brighton main line. The 'Schools' 4-4-0 No 30934 *St Lawrence* will hand the train over to the Standard Class 4 2-6-0, which is waiting to work it over the heavily graded line to Guildford.

Now : 9 January 1996

This picture shows a stopping service from Horsham arriving, whilst to its left unit No 165004 is approaching the platforms with a train from Guildford. On the right of the picture, RES Class 47 *Eastern Star* waits its next turn of duty. *Colin Hogg/Author*

148 BETCHWORTH

Then : 13 August 1960

'4300' and 'Manor' class locomotives from the Western Region had regular workings over the Reading to Redhill line. '4300' class 2-6-0 No 6385 is arriving at Betchworth station with the 4.4pm train to Guildford.

147 REIGATE

Then : 1959
In the last few years of steam working, the Maunsell 'U' and 'N' class 2-6-0s were the regular motive power along this line to Guildford. Here 'N' class No 31815 is crossing the A217 road at the west end of the station.

Now : 9 January 1996
In common with many locations on the Southern not a great deal has changed. Reigate remains the limit of electrification on this picturesque route through the Surrey hills which give the line its modern name. Unit No 166215 is leaving the station, which, for a prestigious town like Reigate, is in a disgracefully neglected condition. *Both Author*

148 BETCHWORTH

Now : 10 January 1996
In contrast to Reigate, the station is smart and well cared for, a particularly pleasing feature being the barley-sugar lamps. A Class 165 unit is passing the well maintained station buildings with a stopping service from Redhill to Reading. The sign below the 'Welcome to Betchworth' proclaims that this is 'The Surrey Hills' (line). *D. B. Clark/Author*

149 DORKING TOWN/DORKING WEST

Then : 1958

On a cold winter afternoon 'N' class 31807 is arriving at Dorking Town with a train from Guildford to Redhill. Station staff are waiting to load a few items into the train. This very pleasant station was situated on the four-mile climb towards Gomshall. This climb, with its ruling gradient of 1 in 96, could tax the locomotives of heavy through trains to the Western Region via Reading General.

Now : 10 January 1996

The station, now known as 'Dorking West', is unmanned. There is little left of the original station, and the goods yard has been taken over by light industry. A Class 37 is passing the station *en route* to Redhill with a short civil engineers train. *Both Author*

The basic waiting shelter, wire fence and stark notice board on the Guildford bound platform hardly reflect the optimistic 'Welcome to Dorking West' sign. *Author*

150 GOMSHALL & SHERE/GOMSHALL

Then : 1958

Western Region 2-6-0 No 6366 has completed the long climb from Deepdene with this westbound through train, and is coasting through the station. Hackhurst Downs is in the background. Before an easy run into Guildford, there is a short ascent through the sandstone hills at Albury Heath.

Now : 10 January 1996

I have taken the train further back than in the 'Then' picture to show the staggered platform layout, and the old brick built signalbox which survived demolition of the station buildings. The former goods yard behind the signalbox is now a caravan sales area. *Both Author*

Way out

151 SHALFORD

Then : 18 July 1964
The station was opened in 1849 and the beautiful station house with its hung tiled elevations, presumably dates from this time. Towards the end of steam working on the line, 'U' class No 31639, hauling a three-coach Bulleid set, is calling at the station with the 6.9pm Redhill to Reading South train. Shortly after leaving the station the line crosses the River Wey before joining the main Portsmouth line at Shalford Junction.

Now : 22 March 1996
The station buildings have gone so that facilities for the passengers are reduced to a minimum. Making a change from the usual diesel units which work the passenger trains, an RES Class 47 diesel-electric locomotive is coming through the station on a parcels train.
Brian Stephenson/Author

153 EARLEY

Then : 23 December 1964
This was the principal intermediate station between Wokingham and Reading South and opened in 1863. It is served by trains on both the Waterloo and Guildford lines, though not all of the latter stopped here in steam days. Standard Class 4 2-6-0 No 76066 is recovering from a signal check with the 12.47pm train from Reading South to Redhill. Diesel-electric units took over the services to Guildford and Redhill in January 1965.

152 WOKINGHAM

Then : 1963

Wokingham is the junction for two routes, the line from Waterloo and Ascot, and the SER route from Ash, which was opened seven years before in 1849. Steam-hauled trains to and from Reading South provided the most interest at Wokingham, such as this stopping service from Redhill and Guildford hauled by 'U' class No 31799 which is pulling out of the station. Note milepost 62¼ at the bottom right hand corner of the picture indicating the mileage from Charing Cross via Redhill and Guildford.

Now : 12 January 1996

The extensive coal yard has been closed in favour of car parking, though it appears to have much spare capacity on this particular day. To the right, light industry has taken over the area once occupied by the goods yard. A train from Guildford to Reading is leaving the station.
Both Author

153 EARLEY

Now : 12 January 1996

Apart from the loss of the signalbox and the semaphore signals, not much has changed over the years. The 14.24 Reading to Waterloo train is entering the station. The train will take about one hour 20 minutes to reach the capital. By contrast, a train from Reading to Paddington on the ex-GWR route, stopping only at Slough, will take about 35 minutes.   *R. L. Sewell/Author*

154 READING SOUTH/READING

Then : 9 June 1954

1903-built South Eastern & Chatham Railway 'D' class 4-4-0 No 31586 from Redhill (75B) shed, engaged on station pilot duty, is a reminder that this was an outpost of the South Eastern Railway. The last survivors of the 'D' class 4-4-0s spent their final years working passenger trains over the 46 mile long line from Redhill and Guildford. The distinctive clock tower of Western Region's Reading General station can be seen above the No 31586's tender. To the right of the locomotive is a glimpse of the platforms of the WR station and ex-GWR lower quadrant signals. The Southern Region station closed in September 1965

Now : 12 January 1996

Nothing remains today of Reading South and the site has been taken over by office accommodation and car parking. A train from Waterloo is standing in the new bay platforms that have been built at the Western Region station. The clock tower can be seen to the right of the edge of the office block. *D. M. C. Hepburne-Scott (Rail Archive Stephenson)/Author*

155 THREE BRIDGES

Then : 18 July 1959

Despite being a busy electrified route, the main line from London to Brighton and the south coast saw a significant number of steam-hauled trains especially at summer weekends. Typical of these is this excursion from Luton on the London Midland Region to Brighton and Hastings, which is being hauled by 'U1' class 2-6-0 No 31890. At this time who would have thought that in the 1990s regular services would operate on this line from Luton and Bedford.

Now : 7 January 1996

Nowadays there is much less variety on this line, though there is still limited through services to Manchester and Glasgow. Other trains to and from the London Midland Region are in the form of Thameslink Bedford and Luton services. One of these is seen leaving the station. *J. Scrace/Author*

Vintage lettering, probably dating from LBSCR days, on the waiting room windows at Three Bridges. *Author*

156 ROWFANT

Then : 1963
Closed on 2 January 1967, Rowfant was on the line from Three Bridges to East Grinstead High Level. The station buildings on the East Grinstead-bound side were surely among the most charming anywhere on the Southern as this picture shows. Push and pull services on the line in the early 1960s were worked by 'H' and 'M7' class 0-4-4Ts based at Three Bridges shed. 'M7' No 30055 has paused at the station with a train from Three Bridges, which it is propelling to East Grinstead.

Now : 7 January 1996
The Worth Way footpath now runs along the course of the line. At Rowfant recent building development and the growth of trees now prevents a proper view of the station which lies abandoned. Surely such a delightful structure deserves a better fate? *Both Author*

157 HORSHAM

Then : 19 July 1959

Horsham was a place of contrasts when this picture was taken. On the one hand electric units passed through frequently on services to and from the Sussex coast. On the other, the steam services to Guildford and Brighton were worked by pre-Grouping locomotives hauling elderly rolling stock. This picture is taken from the road bridge at the London end of the station and shows 'M7' No 30132, from Guildford shed, with the empty stock for the 12.38pm train to Guildford. The line to Dorking curves away to the left from the Three Bridges route by the signalbox. The engine shed, a lovely half roundhouse design, was located out of sight to the right of the signalbox.

Now : 17 January 1996

The track layout is essentially the same and the large goods yard survives. However, with the closure of the lines to Guildford and Brighton in 1965 and 1966 respectively, services using the station are confined to the mid-Sussex line, either from Dorking or Three Bridges and Crawley. Unit No 319019 is arriving with a train from Victoria via Dorking. *J. Scrace/Author*

158 CHRIST'S HOSPITAL

Then : 29 June 1958
The station was opened when the famous school moved here from London, and in its heyday had seven platforms. These served the main mid-Sussex line, and the branches to Brighton (via Itchingfield Junction) and Guildford. 'M7' No 30050 has just arrived at the station with the 9.30am Brighton to Horsham train.

Now : 10 January 1996
Nothing remains of the old station, though the signalbox at the Horsham end survives. Some of the pupils from the school are about to board this stopping train from Portsmouth and Bognor Regis. *J. Scrace/Author*

Below left:
The mid-Sussex line platforms as they were in 1971.

Below:
Detail of the fine brickwork on one of the gable ends of the old station. *Both Author*

159 BAYNARDS TUNNEL

Then : 1957

A few hundred yards south of Baynards station on the line from Guildford and Horsham, lay the short tunnel leading to Rudgwick. It was situated in a deep wooded cutting well illustrated in this picture of 'M7' 0-4-4T No 30056 propelling a train for Horsham into the tunnel.

Now : 23 March 1996

The cutting has been filled in, but the position of the tunnel is now marked by the small round concrete structure in the centre of the picture which presumably gives access for maintenance by means of a shaft. The Downs Link, following the course of the line, goes over the top of the tunnel at this point. *Both Author*

160 CRANLEIGH

Then : 1957

In the 1950s not all trains ran through to Horsham from Guildford. A celebrated train which connected with the 5.50pm train from Waterloo to Portsmouth, was the 6.34pm from Guildford, rostored for an engine off the Redhill to Reading line, sometimes a 'D' class 4-4-0. However, this train is the 1.9pm Saturdays only train from Guildford to Cranleigh, which is arriving at the station behind 'E4' class 0-6-2T No 32505 from Guildford shed. The locomotive, which is hauling a three-coach 'Birdcage' set, will run round the train and return to Guildford at 1.40pm.

Now : 22 March 1996

The site of the station is now occupied by a car park and shops and no trace remains of the railway. The buildings on the right hand side of the picture form the link with the 'Then' view. *Both Author*

161 BRAMLEY & WONERSH

Then : 1960

The first station out of Guildford on the Horsham line, the station was situated between the villages of Bramley and Wonersh. The largest engines seen on the line were probably the 'Q1' class 0-6-0s, and one of these locomotives, No 33001 from Guildford shed, is waiting to leave the station with the 1.9pm train from Guildford to Cranleigh. No 33001 is now owned by the National Railway Museum at York, and is currently based at the Bluebell Railway in east Sussex.

Now : 22 March 1996

The platform on the Horsham-bound side of the station remains as part of the Downs Link long distance footpath between the North and South Downs. The rest of the former station site is occupied by small businesses. *Both Author*

Two of the old station nameboards have been retained at the station, a BR type one and Southern Railway concrete example. This is the former. *Author*

162 WEST GRINSTEAD

Then : undated
Situated between Southwater and Partridge Green on the line between Christ's Hospital and Shoreham, there is of course no connection with East Grinstead, and one wonders whether travellers ever confused the two. One of the Ivatt 2-6-2Ts allocated to the Southern Region, is calling at the station with a train for Horsham.

Now : 23 March 1996
Now on the course of the Downs Link long distance footpath, the southbound platform towards Shoreham is well preserved though only the foundations of the lovely LBSCR built signalbox remain. *David Lawrence/Author*

163 HENFIELD

Then : 6 September 1961
BR Standard Class 2 No 84026 was one of a batch built in 1957 at Darlington for the Southern Region. The locomotive is hauling three Maunsell coaches converted for use as a push and pull set, but not being worked as such. The train is southbound from Horsham to Brighton.

Now : 23 March 1996
The station area has been completely built over and the houses occupy the trackbed. A point of reference is the roof and chimneys of the 'Cat and Canary' public house in Station Road which can be seen in both pictures. *S. C. Creer/Author*

Roads at the sites of closed stations are commonly named after Dr Beeching, and here is the example at Henfield. *Author*

164 BRAMBER

Then : 25 July 1955

After reaching Bramber south of Steyning, the line follows the River Adur closely before joining the coastal route at Shoreham. 'M7' No 30047 hauling a two-coach push and pull set which forms the 4.19pm train from Horsham to Brighton, is coasting into the station.

Now : 23 March 1996

The station has been removed and the trackbed forms part of the Steyning and Bramber bypass. The course of the line is followed by the new road at this point.

Ted Gamblin/Author

165 OLD SHOREHAM

Then : 18 June 1955

'M7' class 0-4-4T No 30053, then shedded at Brighton, has just left the main line at Shoreham and is heading north towards Bramber alongside the River Adur. The level crossing leads to old wooden bridge over the river to the right of the picture. No 30053 was to have an eventful future, for after withdrawal in 1964, was sold to Steamtown in Vermont USA. However, after many years across the Atlantic, it returned to this country and is now based at the Swanage Railway in Dorset. Since then it has travelled on the main line, notably up to Waterloo on a passenger train, and has visited the Bluebell and Mid-Hants railways.

Now : 18 March 1996

The trackbed at this point now forms part of the Downs Link Way. Though the level crossing and signalbox have gone, the rails can still be seen where the track went over the road which led to the old bridge.
Ted Gamblin/Author

The old bridge at Shoreham across the River Adur on 18 March 1996. *Author*

166 MIDHURST

Then : 18 December 1954
This lovely picture was taken on a cold and bright morning not long before closure of the line. 'M7' No 30109 is leaving the station with the 10.40am service from Petersfield to Pulborough. The train was due away from the station at 11.15am after crossing a westbound service from Pulborough to Petersfield. The porter is about to wheel a barrow-load of mail over the line which he will have collected from the Petersfield train.

Now : 27 January 1996
Nothing now remains of this station and the site is occupied by houses. However, behind me, the entrance to the tunnel which was located east of the station, is still visible. *Colin Hogg/Author*

167 ROGATE FOR HARTING

Then : 10 September 1950

This superb picture was taken by E. C. Griffith whose images of trains on this and other lines in the area, are without equal. It shows 'M7' No 30047 leaving the station with the 2.50pm train from Petersfield to Midhurst. This line was opened by the LSWR to its station at Midhurst in 1864. It formed part of the route to Hardham Junction on the mid-Sussex line south of Pulborough. Passenger services were withdrawn between Petersfield and Midhurst in 1955.

Now : 27 January 1996

Almost 46 years on I have to make do with a pheasant on the trackbed! Part of the station building still survives and the platforms can still be made out in the undergrowth.

E. C. Griffith(Courtesy Lens of Sutton)/Author

168 LAVANT

Then : October 1956

The station at Lavant looking north towards Midhurst. This is the sugar beet season and some loaded wagons are awaiting collection. Note the stop block in the third rail from the right. This station, on the line from Midhurst to Chichester, lost its passenger service in 1935.

Now : 24 March 1996

The three-storey station has now been tastefully converted to residential accommodation, and part is used as a nursery school. The trackbed of the line now forms part of the Centurion Way from Chichester to Lavant. *Gerald Siviour/Author*

Detail of the Centurion Way display-board at Lavant. *Author*

169 LEWES

Then : 31 May 1952

Lewes has always been an interesting station from which to watch trains, especially in the days of steam. The present station dates from 1889 and remains largely unaltered. This view is taken from the down platform which serves trains from Haywards Heath to Eastbourne and Hastings. At this time many of the local steam services in the area were still worked by ex-LBSCR locomotives. Two of these are seen here. On the left is 'E5' 0-6-2T No 32571 on the 6.22pm train to Tunbridge Wells West which will travel via Uckfield. To the right, 'E4' class 0-6-2T No 32566 is working the 6.58pm train to Newick and Chailey on the Lewes to East Grinstead line. It will return from Newick at 7.28pm.

Now : 18 March 1996

The single line seen in the last picture has been taken out, otherwise, apart from the removal of the semaphore signals not a great deal has changed. Trains for Seaford (on the left) and Hastings (on the right), are waiting to depart.

J. J. Smith/Author

170 SOUTHERHAM JUNCTION

Then : 1960

At this junction a mile or so south east of Lewes, the line to Newhaven branches off to follow the valley of the River Ouse.

This heavy Saturday through train from the Midlands, hauled by 'N' class 2-6-0 No 31850, is taking the Eastbourne and Hastings line. To the right of the engine, the gate protects the siding into the cement works which was still sending material by rail at this time.

Now : 18 March 1996

The new A27(T) road now crosses the line just north of the junction and its alignment makes an exact repeat picture impossible. The line to the cement works shown in the 1960 picture survives, but is no longer used. It is just out of view to the right. The train is a stopping service for Eastbourne. *Both Author*

171 NEWHAVEN HARBOUR

Then : 24 June 1951
This is the view from the footbridge looking towards the marine terminal and the harbour with the River Ouse to the right of the photographer. A ship from Dieppe is tied up at the quay. The cars waiting by the level crossing have probably been unloaded from the ship by crane. The 5.5pm boat train to Victoria is hauled by 'King Arthur' No 30798 *Sir Hectimere*. To the left a class 2-BIL unit is leaving for Seaford.

Now : 23 March 1996
Cross Channel services still use Newhaven and the Stena Line passenger terminal can be seen on the right of the picture. A service from Seaford to Brighton is passing the site of the old level crossing which can be seen opposite the first and second coaches of the train.
J. J. Smith/Author

172 EASTBOURNE

Then : 16 July 1960
This very interesting and detailed picture shows the 10.40am train from Birmingham Snow Hill approaching the station, where it is due at 3.58pm. The train is composed of GWR and LMS stock and is hauled by 'N' class 2-6-0 No 31862. After reversal the train will go on to Hastings where it is due to arrive at 4.37pm, some six hours after leaving Birmingham. How long would this journey take by car today? Note the Standard 2-6-4T on empty stock and the enormous volume of domestic coal traffic in the yard.

Now: 18 March 1996
With the sharp decline in the use of coal for heating in favour of gas and oil, the yard has been closed and a car sales area now occupies the site. A train from Hastings is approaching the station on this misty morning. *S. C. Nash/Author*

173 BRIGHTON WORKS

Then : 29 September 1956

Brighton works was operational for about 120 years from 1852. Notable among the long line of locomotives built here were Bulleid light pacifics, and nearly all the BR Standard 2-6-4Ts. The works clock shows five past three — some enthusiasts are looking round the erecting shop where this trio of Bulleid pacifics is under repair. They are 'West Country' class Nos 34001 *Exeter*, 34020 *Seaton* and rebuilt 'Merchant Navy' No 35018 *British India Line*. No 35018 was the first of the class to be rebuilt in February 1956.

Now : 18 March 1996

The site of the works is now part of huge car park on the east side of the station. This view is looking south towards the sea.

J. F. Davies (Rail Archive Stephenson)/Author

174 BRIGHTON (1)

Then : undated but c1953

The eastern side of Brighton station looking towards the buffer stops. 'E4' class No 32518 and Ivatt 2-6-2T No 41290 are pulling out of the platform with empty stock made up of LMS coaches, possibly an excursion from the London Midland Region. A class 4-LAV electric unit 'No 2939' is standing in the opposite platform. These units, which were made up of three non-corridor third-class coaches and one 1st/3rd corridor coach, were used mainly on semi-fast services from London to Brighton, and had a reputation for rough riding. To the left of the picture are the offices of the locomotive works.

Now : 18 March 1996

The platforms have been extended but the fine overall roof of the station still remains much as in the original designs of David Moccatta. *Colin Hogg/Author*

The station clock on 18 March 1996. *Author*

175 BRIGHTON (2)

Then : 25 August 1955

The Worthing-bound platforms provided an excellent view of the locomotive shed as is shown by this picture of 'M7' No 30048 arriving with the 1.39pm train from Horsham. Visible in the shed yard is a Standard 2-6-4T which almost certainly will have been built across the tracks in Brighton Works, and a 'C2X' 0-6-0 which was generally employed on local freight duties.

Now : 18 March 1996

The shed has gone with the area now occupied by low rise buildings. *Ted Gamblin/Author*

176 LANCING

Then : 25 July 1955
Lancing was famous for the carriage works which the LBSCR inaugurated in 1908. These finally closed in 1965. One of the powerful and efficient LBSCR 'K' class 2-6-0s No 32339, which was built in 1914, is coasting through the station with an eastbound freight train. Note the neat coal yard behind the train with the lorries waiting to load up with bags of coal for domestic use.

Now : 23 March 1996
The station now enjoys a stopping train every 20 minutes or so on weekdays — here is the 17.44 service from Littlehampton to Brighton about to stop at the station.
Ted Gamblin/Author

178 CHICHESTER

Then : 1946
An early postwar view from the footbridge to the west of the station. 'L12' 4-4-0 No 418, in black livery, is pulling out of the sidings with an empty train composed of GWR stock, possibly bound for Salisbury. No 418 was scrapped in 1951.

177 LITTLEHAMPTON

Then : 24 August 1955

Like Eastbourne and Bognor Regis, Littlehampton is reached by means of a short branch off the main line. Steam-hauled excursions to resorts such as Littlehampton were popular in the pre-1960 period before the advent of widespread car ownership. This excursion, the 6.36pm to Totton near Southampton, which has just left the station, is composed of a vintage rake of ex-LSWR main line stock and hauled by 'U' class 2-6-0 No 31636.

Now : 24 March 1996

Some building development has taken place on the opposite side of the line, but the gas storage site is still in use. A Portsmouth line train is leaving the station.
Ted Gamblin/Author

178 CHICHESTER

Now : 24 March 1996

Apart from the removal of the sidings and new building development, especially to the north of the line, much remains as before. The footbridge continues to provide an excellent view of the trains, such as this departure to Portsmouth. *C. R. L. Coles/Author*

179 WATERLOO (1)

Then : 1965
This is the Victory Arch at Waterloo, which was built as a memorial to the staff of the LSWR who died in World War 1. It forms part of the reconstructed station opened in 1922. The station's impressive façade, viewed from York Road, is marred by the temporary netting on the side wall facing the camera. The Lion has now been moved to Westminster Bridge.

Now : 26 January 1996
Much development work has taken place and the whole area looks a lot tidier, even if the effect is somewhat spoiled by the maze created by the pedestrian barriers. The entry to the station through the Victory Arch gives no hint of the splendours of the new International station waiting inside. *Both Author*

181 VAUXHALL

Then : 1960
The down 'Bournemouth Belle' is passing the station, hauled by an unrebuilt 'West Country' pacific No 34009 *Lyme Regis*, instead of the usual more powerful rebuilt 'Merchant Navy'. No 34009 was rebuilt the following year. The first of the office buildings, which now surround the station, is in course of construction.

Now : 26 February 1996
All the old houses and factories have been swept away, though a space between the new buildings allows sight of the Houses of Parliament. With the opening of the Victoria Line station and the construction of office accomodation in the area, Vauxhall is much busier than it ever was in the 1960s. On the down fast line a Wessex electric is working a service to Southampton. *Both Author*

180 WATERLOO (2)

Then : 1965
The morning rush hour is in full swing with commuters hurrying through the attractive cast-iron gates leading to station concourse. A train from Salisbury has just arrived at platform 14, hauled by No 34004 *Yeovil*. Note the advertisement by the barriers — such is the change in the value of money that £13 would barely buy a good meal in Bournemouth for one, let alone a luxury weekend!

Now : 26 January 1996
Retail outlets are now in the area once occupied by the old gates, rather overshadowing the plain entrances to the platforms. A glimpse of the International station can be seen on the right of the picture. *Both Author*

182 NINE ELMS

Then : 1962

The turntable at Nine Elms (70A) was situated near the Brooklands Street entrance to the shed. 'Q1' No 33001, now part of the National Collection (see page 133 Bramley and Wonersh), and Bournemouth shed's rebuilt 'Merchant Navy' No 35021 *New Zealand Line* have just been turned and are about to move off up the yard.

Now : 7 January 1996

The site of the shed is now occupied by the New Covent Garden Market, the extent of which makes it difficult to pinpoint exactly where pictures in the shed were taken. However, the flats in the background put these two pictures in context, though I have stood further back to give a better idea of the scene today. *Both Author*

184 DURNSFORD ROAD

Then : 1959

Durnsford Road was built to generate electricity for the new LSWR suburban electrification scheme. The chimney on the left is a replacement for the original one hit by a bomb in October 1940. Durnsford Road was closed in 1954 and the chimneys felled in 1965. Prominent among the electric units in the depot are two '4-COR' sets, the leading one being No 3103. On the main line rebuilt Bulleid pacific No 34071 *601 Squadron* is on the 11.15am train from Waterloo to the west of England.

183 CLAPHAM JUNCTION

Then : 7 May 1954
Extensive carriage sidings, for the cleaning and servicing of coaching stock, were located at Clapham Junction between the lines to Windsor and Wimbledon. For many years 'M7' 0-4-4Ts were employed on empty carriage stock duties to and from Waterloo. One of these locomotives, No 30241 shedded at Nine Elms, is entering the sidings with a rake of Pullman coaches which had possibly formed a boat train.

Now : 26 February 1996
The sidings are still in use, mainly to berth electric stock between the morning and evening peak hours. This picture, taken in the late afternoon from the Windsor line platforms, shows one of the empty trains which leave the yard at regular intervals at this time of day to form rush hour trains from Waterloo. During busy periods it is quite easy to see six trains on the move at once, justifying the claim on the new station nameboard on the extreme left of the picture which describes Clapham Junction as Britain's busiest railway station. (see also Clapham Junction Central Section side page 95). *J. Head/Author*

184 DURNSFORD ROAD

Now : 8 December 1995
With the demolition of the old power station and the construction of the new electric unit maintenance depot, the scene from the bridge over the railway has been totally transformed. A Wessex unit is passing with a train for Southampton. *Both Author*

185 NEW MALDEN

Then : 1959

This picture has special significance for me because when I was a child I spent many hours on it watching the trains go by. Rebuilt 'Merchant Navy' No 35024 *East Asiatic Company* is on the up slow line with a train from Bournemouth. Both down lines are shut because of engineering work, probably I think in connection with the reconstruction of the bridge by the station.

Now : 4 November 1995

The view from the bridge has altered very little, and remains a splendid location for photography. The major changes at the station are the demolition of the signalbox and the buildings on the main line platform. A train from the Kingston loop is leaving for Waterloo. *Both Author*

186 CHESSINGTON SOUTH

Then : 13 June 1959

Standard Class 5 4-6-0 No 73088, which has arrived with an excursion from Uxbridge, is berthing its stock in the sidings to the south of the station. The passengers from the train are no doubt visiting what was then Chessington Zoo. To the left is the extensive coal yard, whilst on the right are some of the buildings occupied at that time by the Ordnance Survey. It was planned to extend the line southwards to join the Motspur Park to Dorking line just north of Leatherhead. However, the outbreak of the war in 1939 stopped any further progress beyond Chessington South, though the earthworks survive for a half mile or so beyond the station.

Now : 8 April 1996

The embankment on the west side of the line is very overgrown, so I have had to take the photograph from a slightly different angle to the original picture, if anything is to be seen. The coal depot is still operational, though now served by road and the former Ordnance Survey site is a business park. Chessington South station, located immediately behind the bridge from which this picture is taken, is heavily used during the spring and summer months by visitors to Chessington World of Adventures located on the site of the old zoo.
Terry Gough/Author

187 KINGSTON

Then : 26 June 1937

This picture is almost the only prewar one in the book, but I have included it because of the remarkable similarity to the scene today. The station was rebuilt in the mid-1930s so was almost new when this picture was taken. The flags and bunting on the station are probably to celebrate the Coronation of King George VI. Note the newspaper sellers for *The Star, Evening Standard* and *Evening News* on the far left of the picture, and the trolleybus on route No 602 on the right.

Now : 3 November 1995

After almost 60 years the station is comparatively unaltered even down to the flagpole! Is it the same one? Despite the passage of time the station still looks quite modern, though I feel the oversize British Rail logo sits less comfortably on the frontage than the elegant Southern Railway lettering.
Ian Allan Library/Author

188 TEDDINGTON

Then : 25 March 1962
This was the occasion of a Railway Enthusiasts Club (REC) tour around some southwest London lines using Adams 'O2' 0-4-4T No 30199, which offered the chance to photograph steam in unusual locations. No 30199 has come round the loop from Twickenham *en route* to Kingston. On the other line, a typical local train of the period formed of '4-SUB' unit No 4387, is about to depart.

Now : 18 November 1995
Although lineside vegetation obscures the view of the road in the first photograph, not a great deal has changed at the station, other than the removal of the points and new platform lighting.
Colin Hogg/Author

190 KEW GARDENS

Then : 25 March 1962
The REC tour is seen again (see above at Teddington), this time passing Kew Gardens station on the line from Richmond to Gunnersbury, a route which is shared with District Line and North London line trains.

189 HOUNSLOW

Then : 3 April 1954

It was not that common to see an example of the massive Urie 'G16' 4-8-0Ts out on the main line. They spent most of their time in the marshalling yard at Feltham until the arrival of diesel shunters in the mid-1950s. Here is No 30492 passing Hounslow with a westbound freight probably from Willesden on the London Midland Region. No 30492 was withdrawn at the beginning of 1959, the first of its class to go.

Now : 5 December 1995

Hounslow is now a quiet suburban station with little to break the routine of Waterloo line stopping services which call here every half hour or so during the day. Unit No 5865 is arriving with the 13.22 service to Weybridge.
Colin Hogg/Author

190 KEW GARDENS

Now : 5 December 1995

Some of the attractive station buildings have now been taken over by a pub, and a new section added in Victorian style, loosely based perhaps on the famous hothouses in the nearby Kew Gardens. Whilst the station looks well cared for, it is sad to see the appearance of graffiti not only on the station and bridge, but on the front of the District Line train as well.
Both Author

155

191 FELTHAM MARSHALLING YARD

Then : 1952

A general view, looking east, of the great marshalling yard which was opened not long after World War 1. The control building for the hump yard can be seen just to the right of the smoke from 'H16' No 30520. The engine is about to leave the yard with a westbound freight — note the shunter with his pole between Nos 30520 and 30567. No 30567, an '0395' class 0-6-0, built in 1883, spent the last years of its long career based at Feltham shed for shunting duties in the yard.

Now : 18 November 1995

Like so many similar yards, Feltham is no more, the future for its derelict acres, uncertain. Birch trees and scrub have taken over where miles of sidings and the locomotive shed were once located. On the Reading lines, to the left of the picture, a train for Windsor & Eton Riverside is passing two derelict vans.
C. R. L. Coles/Author

193 VIRGINIA WATER

Then : 27 October 1969

Virginia Water is the junction for the lines to Weybridge and Ascot. This picture shows the 2.28pm train from Waterloo to Reading which is made up of two units, a '2-HAL' leading followed by a '2-BIL'.

Now : 12 January 1996

The 10.26 train from Waterloo to Reading is arriving at the station which looks much the same as before apart from the loss of the signalbox and semaphore signals.
J. Scrace/Author

192 FELTHAM

Then : 5 February 1967

Standard Class 3 No 77014 is passing Feltham West signalbox with the Locomotive Club of Great Britain's 100th rail tour, the South Western Suburban Rail Tour. No 77014 was one of a class of 20 locomotives built at Swindon in 1954 for allocation to the Scottish and North Eastern Regions, No 77014 spending most of its life in the Darlington area. However, at the end of its career, No 77014 was allocated to the Southern Region which withdrew it from service in 1967. None of the class have survived into preservation.

Now : 18 November 1995

The signalbox and level crossing gates have been replaced by automatic lifting barriers overseen by CCTV cameras. A train for Reading is leaving the down platform. *Both Author*

194 WINDSOR & ETON RIVERSIDE

Then : 23 June 1957
'Remembrance' class 4-6-0 No 32331 *Beattie* has just arrived at the impressive 1851-built station with the Ramblers Association special from London Bridge. This train was run in connection with the association's rally at Runnymede.

Now : 12 January 1996
The roof over the platforms has been reduced in length, with the remaining section restored and repainted. The new lighting, designed to be in keeping with the station, looks impressive, though the seats and buffer stops rather detract from the period effect. A train for Waterloo is leaving the station. *Both Author*

The exterior of the station on 12 January 1996.
Author

195 SURBITON

Then : 27 June 1953

The station, originally named Kingston, was opened by the London & Southampton Railway in 1838. The L&S Railway connection is reflected in the 'Southampton Hotel' which can be seen on the right of the picture. The station buildings, including the distinctive clock tower, date from 1937. Salisbury-based 'H15' 4-6-0 No 30334, working an up summer Saturday train, was one of five locomotives constructed in 1925 using parts from earlier Drummond 4-6-0s. No 30334 was withdrawn in June 1958.

Now : 9 December 1995

Nearly 60 years after it was built, the clock tower still stands proud against the rather bland modern buildings to its right. In general the station is largely unaltered, though it would benefit from some general smartening up. The down side booking office has been closed, this area in particular being in need of attention. A train from Portsmouth is passing on the up fast line. *Geoff Rixon/Author*

196 EFFINGHAM JUNCTION

Then : 1952
Steam-hauled trains were not that common on the Guildford New Line other than diversions to avoid engineering work on the main line through Woking. This is a ramblers' excursion to Cranleigh in charge of 'U1' class 2-6-0 No 31904. Note the fine LSWR lower quadrant signals by the bridge, the right hand one controlling the route to Bookham and Leatherhead.

Now : 22 March 1996
The Guildford New Line is still used as a diversionary route. The normal service south of Effingham Junction is made up of trains to and from Victoria and Waterloo via Leatherhead and Surbiton respectively. This is a service from Victoria to Guildford which has just come round the curve off the Leatherhead line.
J. N. Faulkner/Author

197 WEYBRIDGE

Then : June 1953
This lovely picture is taken looking towards London. It shows, from left to right, a '2-NOL' unit after arrival in the up bay with a service from the Virginia Water line; an unrebuilt 'Merchant Navy' No 35010 *Blue Star* on the down 'Devon Belle', and a '2-BIL' unit arriving at the down platform with a stopping train for Woking, Portsmouth and Alton. Patronage of the 'Devon Belle' gradually declined in the early 1950s and it was withdrawn at the end of the 1954 season.

Now : 5 February 1996
There is a new booking office complex on the up side of the station, but otherwise it is remarkably unaltered. A stopping train from Waterloo to Basingstoke, which has just arrived, is making a connection with the service waiting to leave the up bay platform for Addlestone and Virginia Water. *Geoff Rixon/Author*

198 WOKING

Then : 5 June 1970
The distinctive clean cut lines of the Southern Railway-built signalbox dominate this view of the west end of the station (see Ashford International page 57). The 'Warship' class diesel-hydraulic locomotives took over from steam on the Waterloo to Exeter line in the mid-1960s. One of these locomotives, No D819 *Goliath*, is about to leave the station with the 13.08 train from Waterloo to Exeter St David's.

Now : 5 February 1996
Almost 26 years on and virtually nothing has changed but the 'Warships' are only a memory. A Wessex electric unit is waiting to leave with a service to Bournemouth.
J. Scrace/Author

199 FARNBOROUGH

Then : 9 September 1961

The LSWR pneumatically-operated signals controlling the up slow line have already gone back to the 'on' position, even though 'King Arthur' class No 30804 *Sir Cador of Cornwall* has only just passed under the gantry with its train for Waterloo. The locomotive still retains a six-wheeled tender fitted for use on the Central Section. No 30804, which was then shedded at Eastleigh, had only a few months of life remaining before withdrawal in February 1962.

Now : 5 February 1996

The LSWR signals went in the mid-1960s, but apart from the loss of the roof on the footbridge and the extension to the platform, the scene looks much the same. Farnborough is a busy commuter station, also serving the many firms that have set up offices in the area.
Colin Hogg/Author

201 BASINGSTOKE

29 May 1961

The London & Southampton Railway reached Basingstoke in 1839, to be joined by the Great Western route from Reading nine years later in 1848. It has always been an important junction, not only for freight traffic to and from the Midlands, but also for inter-Regional passenger trains, especially those which ran on summer Saturdays in the 1950s and 1960s. As befitted its status there were extensive marshalling yards and a locomotive shed (70D). 'S15' 4-6-0 No 30513 is pulling slowly out of the yard, past the shed, with a long freight train, probably bound for Feltham.

200 WINCHFIELD

Then : 15 April 1949

A fine view of the station looking east. 'King Arthur' 4-6-0 No 30777 *Sir Lamiel* in early BR livery is on the down fast line with a train for Bournemouth which includes some Urie 'Ironclad' coaches.

Now : 5 February 1996

Nothing now remains of the attractive buildings to the west of the station and the goods yards on both sides of the line have closed. A stopping train for Basingstoke is leaving the station.

E. C. Griffith(Courtesy Lens of Sutton)/Author

201 BASINGSTOKE

Now : 14 April 1996

Basingstoke has developed from a small market town to a significant business centre. Many large new office developments now surround the station which offers an excellent service of trains not only on the London, Southampton and Salisbury lines, but also to Reading and the Midlands. On this Sunday afternoon a Wessex electric is arriving with the late running 12.34 train to Waterloo, delayed by a lineside fire in the Southampton area.

R. S. Greenwood/Author

202 FARNHAM

Then : December 1960

It is just before Christmas 1960 on a dull and cold December afternoon. 'M7' 0-4-4T No 30132 shedded at Guildford, has just arrived at the station with a Christmas parcels train. The locomotive is carrying the Waterloo to Southampton via Alton disc code. In the 1950s and early 1960s the Christmas period offered a welcome opportunity to see interesting locomotives on these special workings (see also Cheam page 117).

Now : 2 March 1996

Apart from the loss of the goods yard, few changes of note have taken place to enliven the routine of the electric service to and from London. Unit No 3430 has just arrived with the late running 10.42 train from Waterloo. *Both Author*

204 BORDON

Then : 1958

Bordon was the interchange point for the Longmoor Military Railway whose sidings can just be seen to the right of the fine LSWR bracket signal which controlled entry to the station. 'U' class No 31616 has worked a freight train down the branch from Bentley and is being serviced prior to its return.

203 BENTLEY

Then : undated but c1956

Bentley was the junction for the 4¾ mile long branch to Bordon, which closed to passengers in 1957. Complete closure followed in 1966. 'M7' No 30027 from Guildford shed, which supplied locomotives to work the branch, is waiting to leave the down side bay platform. On the left of the picture, a train from Alton *en route* to Waterloo has just arrived.

Now : 2 March 1996

The down line has now been taken out of use so all trains, such as this service to Alton, call at the up platform. To the right, the bay which once housed the Bordon branch trains is still visible, but the trackbed is very overgrown. *N. C. Simmons/Author*

204 BORDON

Now : 2 March 1996

Nothing remains of the station or the yard, and the site is now an industrial estate. This is the view taken looking down the line of the trackbed towards Bentley, and is as close as I can get to the position from where I took the original picture. *Both Author*

205 ALTON

Then : 2 April 1969
Trains for Winchester and Fareham used platforms 2 and 3 at Alton, whilst platform 1 was generally reserved for the electric service to Waterloo. Hampshire diesel unit No 1105 is waiting to leave platform 2 with the 3.2pm service to Winchester and Southampton.

Now : 3 February 1996
Mid-Hants Railway trains now have exclusive use of platform 3 where David Shepherd's '9F' 2-10-0 No 92203 is arriving with a train from Alresford. Class 58 diesel No 58040 *Cottam Power Station* is standing in platform 2 before running light to Holybourne oil depot to pick up a train. *J. Scrace/Author*

207 ROPLEY

Then : 15 May 1966
When this picture was taken Ropley was just a quiet country station, but clearly there was room for the developments that would come with the Mid-Hants Railway in the late 1970s. London Midland Region Class 5 No 45493 is on the Sunday 8.55am Bournemouth to Waterloo train diverted from the main line because of engineering works. It will return from Waterloo at 8.30pm. The engine has worked south with the York to Poole train on the previous day and has been 'borrowed' for this duty to Waterloo.

206 MEDSTEAD & FOUR MARKS

Then : 27 July 1957
Medstead & Four Marks station is situated at the end of a long climb from Alresford which could severely tax heavily loaded through trains diverted off the main Winchester to Basingstoke line. Most of the local services between Eastleigh and Alton were worked by push and pull fitted 'M7' class 0-4-4Ts. However, No 30041, on the 3.59pm Eastleigh to Alton train, made up of two LSWR coaches, was not so fitted. After leaving the station No 30041 will pass through a deep chalk cutting before making an exhilarating descent into Alton.

Now : 14 March 1995
After closure of the line by British Railways in 1973, the first section of the preserved line between Alresford and Ropley was opened by the Mid-Hants Railway (the Watercress Line) in 1977, and now extends through to Alton. The visit of 'M7' No 30053 from the Swanage Railway was an opportunity to recreate a typical Winchester to Alton train of the 1950s. No 30053 has been renumbered as '30479', an Eastleigh-based 'M7' which regularly worked on the line in the 1950s. The new signal box is from Wilton South. I even have 'Then and Now' signalmen in the photographs!
Antony Linaker/Author

207 ROPLEY

Now : 2 March 1996
The scene at Ropley has been transformed by the construction of the locomotive shed and workshop in the old station yard. At the station, the up side platform is fully operational and a footbridge has been installed. Visiting 'A4' class No 60007 *Sir Nigel Gresley* is on a train for Alresford. Although this class did not work through here in BR days, 'A4s' did appear on special trains on the main line to Bournemouth, including this locomotive, then numbered 4498 and painted in LNER livery. *J. Scrace/Author*

208 ALRESFORD

Then : Summer 1957
This peaceful view of the station is taken looking east towards Alton. A boarded crossing at the far end of the station links the two platforms. At this time there were about nine trains on weekdays and four on Sundays, in each direction.

Now : 4 February 1996
All Mid-Hants Railway stations now have footbridges to link the two platforms, but at the time of writing the one at Medstead has yet to be commissioned. This view is taken from the new footbridge and shows that the essential features of the station have been retained. Obvious differences other than the footbridge, are the lengthened platform on the up side and the new refreshment room between the station house and the signalbox. *Both Author*

209 WEST MEON

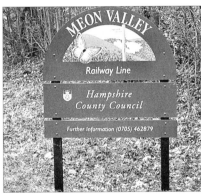

Then : 13 November 1954
The greatly-mourned Meon Valley line was closed to passengers in February 1955. The occasion was marked by a very successful special train, 'The Hampshireman' run by the Railway Correspondence & Travel Society on 6 February. It was hauled up the line behind two 'T9' class 4-4-0s, Nos 30301 and 30732. In the picture, taken a month or two before closure, another 'T9', No 30726 is pausing at this lovely station with the 10.20am freight from Alton to Fareham.

Left:
South of the station site, the trackbed has been cleared to form the Meon Valley Railway Line Path. This is the sign at West Meon. *Author*

Now : 2 March 1996
Yes, this really is the same place, bringing to mind the ruins of some lost city in the jungle. Because of the growth of trees and scrub, this is the best view I could obtain of the old northbound platform which is shown behind the 'T9' in the other picture. *J. J. Smith/Author*

210 WICKHAM

Then : 1958
Wickham was the first station out of Fareham on the Meon Valley line. By the time this picture was taken, the line had been closed to passenger traffic. 'U' class 2-6-0 No 31637 is working a pick-up freight to Alton.

Now : 2 February 1996
Some concrete fence posts are all that remain to identify the location of the station situated on the southeastern edge of the village. The site is very overgrown so this is the best view I could secure looking towards Fareham.
Gerald Siviour/Author

211 FAREHAM

Then : 19 April 1954
Drummond '700' class 0-6-0 No 30308 is
waiting to leave the station with the 6.48pm
train to Alton where it is due at 7.46pm. In
1954 only four trains per day used the line in
each direction, this being the last northbound
service.

Now : 24 March 1996
The site of the bay platform used by the Meon
Valley line trains is now part of the station car
park. On the right a diverted InterCity train
has paused briefly in the station.
Colin Hogg/Author

212 GUILDFORD

Then : 3 April 1966
This picture is taken from the footbridge which
spans the lines at the north end of the station.
Dimly seen on the left in the background is the
chalk cliff under which the Guildford's half
roundhouse locomotive shed (70C) was located.
'U' class 2-6-0 No 31639 and 'N' class 2-6-0
No 31411 are departing for Salisbury, via
Reading and Basingstoke, with the Locomotive
Club of Great Britain (LCGB) 'Wilts and Hants'
railtour.

Now : 22 March 1996
Happily it is still possible to photograph steam
at Guildford. This is one of the round trips from
Victoria via Redhill, Guildford and Woking.
The luncheon train is hauled by rebuilt
'Merchant Navy' No 35028 *Clan Line*. The site
of the shed is now a multi-storey car park which
can be seen above the fifth to seventh coaches
behind the locomotive. *Brian Stephenson/Author*

213 GODALMING GOODS

Then : 21 January 1959
The old station at Godalming closed to passengers in 1897, and to freight traffic in 1969. In this picture, a special train, commemorating the opening of the direct line to Portsmouth in 1859, has arrived at the station behind Drummond '700' class 0-6-0 No 30350.

Now : 8 November 1995
This is Old Station Road, the name being the only reminder of the buildings which once stood here. The pine trees in the background provide another link with the past.
Both Author

214 PETERSFIELD

Then : undated but probably early 1950s
Petersfield was the junction for the branch to Midhurst opened in 1864, and closed in 1955 (see also Rogate page 139). The Midhurst line had its own bay platform on the other side of the level crossing to the north of the main station. A push and pull train hauled by an 'M7' 0-4-4T is waiting to leave for Midhurst.

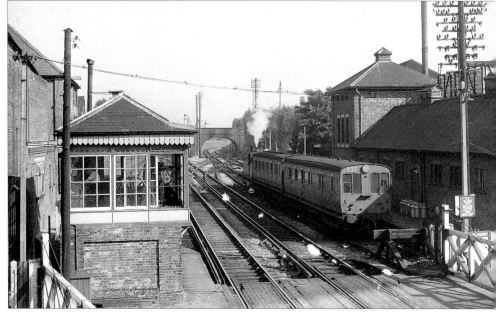

Now : 14 January 1996
The signalbox controlling the busy level crossing survives but there is no trace of the simple wooden Midhurst line platform. However, the course of the closed branch through the right hand arch of the bridge in the background is still clearly discernible. *Ian Allan Library/Author*

215 ROWLANDS CASTLE

Then : 20 August 1969
'4-COR' unit No 3109 is passing the station with the 12.20pm Portsmouth Harbour to Waterloo train. The units forming the train will be working hard on the eastbound climb from Havant to Buriton, which later steepens to 1 in 80. After the summit the line descends through Buriton tunnel towards Petersfield.

Now : 14 January 1996
The signal box has gone but the station looks well cared for. Unit No 1884 is working the 12.13 train from Portsmouth Harbour to Waterloo. The down line repeater signal is now in use on the gantry seen in the previous picture. *J. Scrace/Author*

216 LANGSTON (1)

Then : 1961

This is the level crossing across the main road from Havant to
Hayling Island. A train for Havant has just left the halt at Langston
hauled by 'Terrier' 0-6-0T No 32670. This locomotive is now based
at Rolvenden on the Kent & East Sussex Railway. The cars waiting at
the crossing, are also of interest. One is a Morris 1000 Traveller, and
the other, I think, a Wolesley 6/90. The chalked message on the
concrete level crossing post reads 'DLJ 727 your number plate in
here'— the arrow points to the house.

Now : 14 January 1996

The road has now been doubled in width, though the attractive
weather-boarded house has been spared. *Both Author*

217 LANGSTON (2)

Then : 1961
The Hayling Island branch closed in November 1963. Its principal feature was the wooden bridge across the channel at Langston harbour. 'Terrier' class 0-6-0T No 32661 has just crossed the bridge on its way to Hayling Island. In the middle is the small signalbox controlling the section of the bridge that could be moved to allow the passage of high-masted boats. On the right is the road bridge to Hayling Island which offered a splendid view of the railway especially towards sunset when the trains were silhouetted against the sky.

Now : 14 January 1996
The metal signal post still stands guard over the southern approach to the bridge. The remains of the piers, and the section of the bridge where the signalbox was located, are also visible. *Both Author*

218 HAYLING ISLAND

Then : 12 May 1956
The 4½ mile long branch from Havant to
Hayling Island was opened in 1867. The
intensive service of trains was worked by the
ex-LBSCR 'Terrier' class 0-6-0Ts from Fratton
shed. One of these, No 32640, has just arrived
with the 12.35pm train from Havant, and is
being admired by two smartly dressed boys,
perhaps at the start of a holiday. No 32640 is
now on the Isle of Wight Steam Railway (see
Haven Street page 187).

Now : 14 January 1996
Sadly the station has been completely
demolished though its memory lingers on
through the survival of the goods shed and in
the name of the new theatre which is being
built on the site. *Ian Allan Library/Author*

The station in 1960 looking towards the buffer
stops and showing the other end of the goods
shed. *Author*

219 PORTSMOUTH & SOUTHSEA

Then : 5 August 1955

The impressive terminal station, seen behind push and pull fitted 'O2' Class 0-4-4T No 30207, dates from 1876. This picture is taken from the high level platforms served by trains on the line to the Harbour station. On this hot summer afternoon passengers waiting for a train from the Harbour have little else to do other than watch No 30207 shunting some vans.

Now : 14 January 1996

By a strange coincidence the station clock shows the same time as it did in the 1955 picture! Although the high level part of the station has been modernised, demolition of the office block has opened up the view of the terminal building. That part of the station now mainly handles trains to Fareham and along the south coast route to Brighton. *Ted Gamblin/Author*

220 PORTSMOUTH HARBOUR

Then 10 August 1963
Steam locomotives could regularly be seen at the Harbour station on scheduled services in the summer holiday season. This is the 9.11am Portsmouth Harbour to Wolverhampton Low Level train hauled by Standard Class 5 No 73114 *Etarre*. The front three coaches are ex-LMS stock.

Now : 14 January 1996
The buildings of the Royal Naval Dockyard and the tall masts of HMS *Warrior*, are prominent in the background of this picture. The train is the 15.24 to Exeter St David's, via Southampton and Salisbury, which is scheduled to arrive at Exeter at 18.12.
S. Creer/Author

221 RYDE ESPLANADE

Then : 1964

No 32 *Bonchurch* has just left the station and is about to enter the 391yd long Ryde tunnel with a train for Ventnor. The large collection of coaches and buses parked by the station is a reminder of the importance of the tourist industry to the Isle of Wight. On peak Saturdays in the 1950s, up to five trains an hour would leave Ryde Pier Head, some running non-stop to Brading or Sandown.

Now : 4 March 1996

At the time this picture was taken, the southbound line from the Pier Head to the Esplanade station was not operational, so trains for Shanklin were using the crossover seen behind the Class 483 unit. This picture shows how the line turns sharply through the station before running on to the pier. *Both Author*

222 RYDE ST JOHN'S ROAD

Then : 1962
The railway works and the main shed were located at Ryde St John's. A locomotive in the shed yard can just be seen to the right of the picture. The fireman of 'O2' No 29 *Alverstone* is about to hand over the single line token to the waiting signalman.

Now : 4 March 1996
Externally at least, the signalbox is largely unaltered, and some of the area once occupied by the shed is taken up by a car park. One of the ex-London Transport Class 483 units is working a Shanklin to Ryde Pier Head service. The line on the extreme left of the picture leads into the works area. *Both Author*

Detail of the cast-iron Isle of Wight Railway monogram at the station on 4 March 1996. *Author*

225 WROXALL

Then : 1963
The fireman of No 35 *Freshwater*, on this train from Ryde, has just handed over the single line tablet to the signalman at Wroxall. The line continues to climb from the station to the 1,312yd long Ventnor tunnel.

Now : 4 March 1996
The old factory building and the overbridge remain as clear points of reference, but even so it is difficult to believe the railway once ran through here. *Both Author*

226 VENTNOR

Then : 19 April 1959

A lovely detailed view of the station looking towards the tunnel and St Boniface Down. No 30 *Shorwell* is about to run round its train. Some of the cars in the forecourt are probably taxis which would have been well used since the station was situated high above the main part of the town.

Now : 4 March 1966

The line from Shanklin to Ventnor closed in 1966 and the site of the station is now an industrial estate. The blocked off tunnel, visible in the centre of the picture, is owned by Southern Water.

J. Spencer Gilks/Author

228 MERSTONE

Then : 1955

Merstone was an isolated station situated to the south of the village. This 'O2' 0-4-4T has stopped at the station with a train from Newport and will proceed to Sandown once the signalman and fireman have exchanged the single line tokens. The line from Newport to Sandown closed in February 1956.

227 VENTNOR WEST

Then : Summer 1952

No W36 *Carisbrooke* is taking water at the far end of the station before making the 6¾ mile journey to Merstone. Judging by the angle of the shadows, the engine could be about to work the 11.57am train. The station was situated some distance from the centre of the town, so it is not surprising that the line was an early closure, services ending in September 1952.

Now : 4 March 1996

The area once occupied by the station has been built over, but the station house, seen on the left hand side of the picture, has been saved. It is now a private residence.
J. N. Faulkner/Author

228 MERSTONE

Now : 4 March 1996

Nothing remains of the station other than the platform surfaces concealed under the grass and scrub. However, the pine trees which gave some protection to this exposed station, are still there. *Terry Gough/Author*

229 ASHEY

Then : 5 June 1961

Ashey was a small isolated station between Haven Street and Smallbrook Junction. It saw most use when the nearby race track was open in the 1920s. By the time this picture was taken the station was beginning to look neglected. There are probably no passengers for the 2.18pm train from Ryde Pier Head to Cowes which is hauled by No 24 *Calbourne*.

Now : 3 March 1996

Although the Ryde to Cowes line closed in 1966, the section east of Wootton was preserved and Isle of Wight Steam Railway trains still call by request at Ashey. The station house itself has been converted to a private residence.

K. L. Cook (Rail Archive Stephenson)/Author

The footpath sign at Ashey station. *Author*

230 HAVEN STREET

Then : 5 June 1961

The station, which served the small village nearby, consisted of an island platform and a 1920s-built booking office. No 24 *Calbourne*, which was destined to be the only 'O2' class 0-4-4T to survive, is about to leave the station with the 3.31pm train from Cowes to Ryde Pier Head.

Now : 3 March 1996

Haven Street is now the headquarters of the Isle of Wight Steam Railway which runs trains between Wootton and a new station at Smallbrook Junction. Smallbrook provides a connection with electric services on the Ryde to Shanklin line. I have moved back further from the point where the original picture was taken, and used a wide angle lens, to show the extent of the new facilities. These include an engine shed and workshop. No 8 *Freshwater*, the one-time No 32646, is on the left of the picture. *K. L. Cook (Rail Archive Stephenson)/Author*

231 NEWPORT

Then : 1964

Shortly after leaving the station, No 17 *Seaview* is crossing the River Medina on this miserable wet afternoon, with a train for Ryde. The MG 1300 and Morris 1000 cars are almost as interesting as the train!

Now : 3 March 1996

The Newport by-pass now crosses the river on almost the same alignment as the railway once did. Although the warehouse on the left of the picture appears to be in far worse condition than it was in the 1960s, the quay looks well cared for. With the disappearance of local industries, such as the importation of timber seen in the earlier picture, the attractive workaday appearance of the old quay has been lost. *Both Author*

233 FRESHWATER

Then : 10 September 1953

A few days before closure on 21 September, No 33 *Bembridge* has arrived at the station with a train from Newport, 12 miles distant. Possibly the bus to the right of the locomotive is forming an onward connection to Totland Bay.

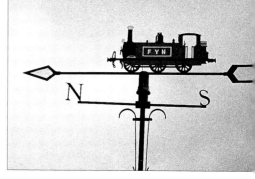

232 COWES

Then : 1958
The terminus at Cowes looking towards the buffer stops. No 17 *Seaview* is waiting to leave the station with a train for Newport and Ryde.

Now : 3 March 1996
The station area has now been cleared, most of the site being occupied by the Admiral Gardens luxury apartments out of sight to the left of the picture. The principal point of reference in both pictures is the roof of the Catholic church in Terminus Road. *Both Author*

233 FRESHWATER

Now : 3 March 1996
The site of the station is now shared between a shop, its car park and a garden centre. Sections of the station boundary fence and parts of the concrete station nameboards are still visible on the site. The house on the right is the common factor in both pictures. *R. C. Riley/Author*

The weather vane in the garden centre features a Freshwater & Yarmouth and Newport Railway 'Terrier' class locomotive. *Author*

234 WORTING JUNCTION

Then : 1963

The lines to Southampton and Salisbury divide at Worting Junction, the latter passing under the up Southampton line at Battledown flyover. This is the view at the junction looking west. Unrebuilt 'Battle of Britain' pacific No 34065 *Hurricane*, working a train to the Midlands, has just crossed the flyover and shut off steam for the approach to Basingstoke, some two miles distant. The tracks from left to right are: down Southampton, down Salisbury, up Salisbury, up Southampton.

Now : 14 April 1996

Apart from the removal of the signalbox and semaphore signals, made redundant by the advent of modern colour light signalling, there have been some changes to the track layout to allow higher speed running through the junction. A Class 159 unit is working a Portsmouth to Reading service. *Both Author*

236 WINCHESTER

Then : 1963

Rebuilt 'Merchant Navy' No 35014 *Nederland Line* is coasting through the station with the down 'Bournemouth Belle', due at Southampton Central at 1.58pm. The gradient post in front of the picturesque ganger's hut is a reminder that after reaching Litchfield tunnel, the crew of the locomotive could enjoy a downhill run all the way to St Denys on the outskirts of Southampton.

235 MICHELEDEVER

Then : 1964

Micheldever station is situated on the long climb from St Denys, on the outskirts of Southamptom, to Litchfield tunnel. Rebuilt 'West Country' pacific No 34013 *Okehampton* is on an express for Waterloo. It will shortly pass the extensive stock sidings that were located on the down side of the line, before entering the first of the two short Popham tunnels.

Now : 4 December 1995

Now that the four tracks which once ran through the station have been reduced to two, trains stop at a new island platform located next to what used to be the fast lines. A Class 159 unit is about to call at the station with the 11.45 service to Reading. *Both Author*

236 WINCHESTER

Now : 24 March 1996

Because of the growth of lineside trees, I have had to move round slightly for this picture which shows the 10.00 train for Portsmouth Harbour. The most obvious change is the lengthening of the station platforms. *Both Author*

237 EASTLEIGH

Then : 1 August 1957
The scene at Eastleigh looking north towards the station was taken from Campbell Road which led to the works and shed. 'King Arthur' No 30783 *Sir Gillimere* is slowly passing through on a freight train for Southampton Docks. The carriage works is located in the middle distance, beyond the rake of coaches berthed by the line to Fareham.

Now : 4 December 1995
With so much goods traffic now carried by road, it is pleasing to be able to photograph two freight trains simultaneously. On the left is a tanker train from Fawley, whilst on the right a Crompton Class 33 diesel is in charge of a consignment of commercial vehicles.
Ian Allan Library/Author

239 CHANDLERS FORD

Then : May 1956
This beautiful picture was taken from the road bridge to the east of the station, which was situated on the line between Romsey and Eastleigh. 'M7' No 30479 from Eastleigh shed is working a train from Andover to Eastleigh composed of two LSWR coaches. Unlike many other 'M7s', No 30479 was not fitted with push and pull gear. Rather unusually for the time of year, it is carrying a snow plough. (see also Medstead & Four Marks page 167)

238 EASTLEIGH WORKS

Then: undated but circa mid 1950s

With the closure of the old works at Nine Elms, the new LSWR locomotive works at Eastleigh was opened in 1909. This is the erecting shop showing 'West Country' class No 34034 *Honiton* from Plymouth shed undergoing overhaul. By the standards of today everything looks a little haphazard, especially the use of the long ladder to gain access to the top of the locomotive. No 34034 was rebuilt in 1960.

Now : 4 December 1995

Apart from the installation of modern equipment, the appearance of the old erecting shop is essentially the same. The works now undertakes a variety of repairs for the three rolling stock companies.
John Ashman FRPS/Author (Courtesy Wessex Traincare Ltd.)

239 CHANDLERS FORD

Now : 23 March 1996

This must be one of the most depressing pictures in the book. The Romsey to Eastleigh line, which has now been singled, was closed to passenger traffic in 1969. Only the remains of the platform are visible as a reminder of this once lovely location. *Gerald Siviour/Author*

240 DUNBRIDGE

Then : 1958

The station is situated on the 1847-built line between Salisbury and Eastleigh, just west of the former Kimbridge Junction where the line to Andover diverged. 'H15' No 30476 from Eastleigh shed is coasting through the station with a freight from Salisbury. No 30473, which was built in 1924, was withdrawn in August 1959 after an uneventful but useful career.

Now : 3 April 1996

Happily the station was undergoing some renovation work at the time of my visit. A Class 150 unit has just drawn to a halt with the 15.10 train to Southampton Central. *Both Author*

241 BISHOP'S WALTHAM

Then : 1962
The station was located at the end of the short branch from Botley opened in 1863. The passenger services were withdrawn early on in 1933, but goods traffic continued to use the line until 1962. Ivatt 2-6-2T No 41328 has just arrived from Botley and is shunting some wagons of coal. The local coal merchant's lorry can be seen to the right of No 41328.

Now : 25 March 1996
The site of the station is now a roundabout at the junction of the B2177 and B3035 roads. The level crossing gates, which can be glimpsed through the trees on the far left of the picture, have been preserved and mark the start of the Bishop's Waltham Railway Path, whilst the building on the right is now a Little Chef restaurant. *Gerald Siviour/Author*

One of the information boards at the start of the railway path. Curiously an Isle of Wight 'O2' has been chosen for the picture, since 'M7' 0-4-4Ts were more usual on the freight trains in the branch's last years of operation. *Author*

195

242 FORT BROCKHURST

Then : 27 June 1950

Fort Brockhurst was the intermediate station of the one-time LSWR main line between Fareham and Gosport. The final sparse passenger service over the five-mile line was withdrawn in 1953. Here 'L12' 4-4-0 No 30420 has little work to do with a two-coach train to Gosport.

Now : 24 March 1996

The station house and the remains of the southbound platform can just be seen in this view looking towards Fareham.
R. C. Riley collection/Author

243 GOSPORT

Then : 3 May 1953

Just before closure in June 1953, a Stephenson Locomotive Society railtour has arrived at the station. The train consists of 'M7' 0-4-4T No 30110 sandwiched between two push and pull sets. The impressive building was designed by Sir William Tite and opened in 1841. A spur to a private royal station at Clarence Yard was brought into use in 1844, and used by Queen Victoria for her journeys to Osborne House on the Isle of Wight.

Now : 24 March 1996

Sadly the station, which is now a listed building, had been allowed to become rather derelict in recent years. However, the site has been tidied and fenced off, and the Architects Department of the Hampshire County Council, have started renovation work. *Ian Allan Library/Author*

Inset : The sign outside The Railway Inn by the station depicting an arrival of Queen Victoria by train. *Author*

244 NETLEY

Then : 1956
One of the beautiful LBSCR Atlantics, No 32425 *Trevose Head*, which has been smartly turned out by Brighton shed, is passing the station with a through train from Bournemouth to Brighton. The signal on the left hand side of the picture controls entry to the short branch that was opened by the LSWR to serve the Victoria Military Hospital.

Now : 25 March 1996
Since I could not stand on the lineside as in the earlier picture, I have had to come further forward on to the platform. A train for Portsmouth is arriving at this well maintained station. The branch to the hospital has now been lifted. *Gerald Siviour/Author*

245 SWANWICK

Then : 1956
As late as 1956 pure LSWR trains could still be seen in the Southampton area. This stirring picture shows 'T9' No 30117 hard at work on the 1 in 81 gradient through the station with a football excursion from Southampton to Portsmouth.

Now : 24 March 1996
Smooth and fast running this Class 158 unit may be, but it has none of the visual impact of the 'T9'. The train is the 17.31 from Southampton Central to Portsmouth Harbour. *Gerald Siviour/Author*

246 ST DENYS

Then : May 1958
Western Region locomotives had a number of duties which brought them into Southampton, such as Churchward '4300' class 2-6-0 No 5345 on a train from the Didcot Newbury & Southampton line. The fine signal gantry controlled trains on the lines from Eastleigh and Fareham which converged at St Denys. To the left of the picture, one of the then new Hampshire diesel units is on a northbound service.

Now : 25 March 1996
The station remains remarkably unchanged, retaining its long footbridge over both sets of lines. Because the main station building on the left has now been leased as office accommodation, the booking office is located on the centre platform. *Gerald Siviour/Author*

247 MOUNT PLEASANT

Then : 1966
It is a hot summer afternoon at this crossing situated between Northam and St Denys. Particularly in those more unhurried days, a level crossing was something of a meeting place allowing time for a chat while waiting for the train to pass. This Waterloo express is in charge of rebuilt 'West Country' No 34095 *Brentor*.

Now : 25 March 1996
The gates have given way to lifting barriers which are sited further back than the old crossing. A Class 47 diesel-electric locomotive is accelerating a heavy container train from Southampton docks towards St Denys and Eastleigh. Compared to the 1966 view, the goods yard on the down side of the line is virtually empty save for a few civil engineers wagons. *Both Author*

248 SOUTHAMPTON TERMINUS

Then : 1960
Standard Class 4 2-6-0 No 76053, seen in this picture leaving the station with a train of empty stock, was the first of a batch of 17 built at Doncaster for the Southern Region. It is fitted with a BR1B tender. Southampton Terminus station closed completely in 1968, but at the time this picture was taken, liners were still using the old Docks, part of which can be seen on the right. Entrance to the docks, using the crossing over Canute Road, was from a line on the down side of the station, ie on the left hand side of the picture.

Now : 25 March 1996
The whole area has been redeveloped for housing, but a link with the past is a glimpse of the terminal building by the station on the extreme right side of both pictures.
Both Author

249 SOUTHAMPTON TOWN QUAY

Then : 5 October 1957
For many years shunting on the Town Quay situated between the Terminus station and the Royal Pier was carried out by the diminutive 'C14' 0-4-0Ts. These Drummond-designed locomotives were originally constructed as 2-2-0 motor train tank engines, but were rebuilt by Urie as 0-4-0T shunters. No 30588 was almost at the end of its long career when this picture was taken, for it was withdrawn in December 1957.

Now : 23 March 1996
Whilst the buildings surrounding the old Terminus station are unchanged, the rails have been lifted and the area is used for car parking.
Colin Hogg/Author

250 SOUTHAMPTON ROYAL PIER

Then : 26 April 1962
A short distance further west from Town Quay is the Royal Pier. 'USA' tank No 30069, one of a number which were based at Southampton Docks shed (71I), is shunting wagons near the entrance to the pier. Note the road sign on the right-hand side of the picture showing London 78 miles. The cranes bordering the New Docks can be seen behind the wagons.

Now : 23 March 1996
The location is still clearly recognisable but there is nothing to remind a passer-by that trains once worked here. *Colin Hogg/Author*

251 SOUTHAMPTON CENTRAL

Then : 1963

The pleasing clock tower of the old station dominates this view of rebuilt Bulleid pacific No 34017 *Ilfracombe* leaving with a train for Waterloo. Grease and oil from engines waiting to depart tended to make the rails very slippery at this point. Close examination of the driving wheels of No 34017 will show that the engine has momentarily lost its feet.

Now : 23 March 1996

The station has been completely rebuilt, and though efficient and busy, there is none of the drama of steam age departures. One of the sleek Wessex electric units is leaving the station for Waterloo.
Both Author

252 MARCHWOOD

Then : 1956
Passenger services were withdrawn over the Fawley branch in February 1966. At the time this picture was taken, passenger services were very sparse, the primary traffic being to the MoD depot at Marchwood and the oil refinery at Fawley. The picture shows 'M7' No 30375 leaving the station with a three-coach ex-LSWR set bound for Southampton.

Now : 23 March 1996
This location provided me with the greatest surprise during my travels as the station looks basically untouched from the 1960s. The level crossing gates have, however, been renewed, and a second track added through the station, controlled by new signals. *Gerald Siviour/Author*

Inset : A close-up of the once so familiar traditional Southern concrete lamp standard and lamp shade. Such fittings have, so far as I know, long vanished from all other stations on the network. *Author*

253 BEAULIEU ROAD

Then : 1966

Towards the end of steam in July 1967, local services between Southampton and Bournemouth were largely handled by the BR Standard locomotives such as No 76016. This was one of a batch built at Horwich in 1953 for the Southern Region which allocated them to Eastleigh where they proved to be useful and reliable. Four examples of the class have survived, including No 76017 which can now be seen on the Mid-Hants Railway.

Now : 9 March 1996

On this gloomy afternoon, unit No 1889, working a stopping service from Southampton to Brockenhurst, represents the modern equivalent of No 76016's train. Beaulieu Road station, now unmanned, is located in the heathland midway between the villages of Beaulieu and Lyndhurst. *Both Author*

254 BROCKENHURST

Then : c1966
Brockenhurst was the junction for the lines to
Lymington Pier and Ringwood. A railtour,
which has just been down to Lymington behind
Standard tank No 80151, is arriving back in the
up main line platform. To the left another
Standard tank is about to propel the Lymington
branch train into the platform.

Now : 9 March 1996
The extensive sidings that were on the down
side of the line have been lifted and the area
used for car parking. The train is one of the
regular InterCity workings which use this route,
the 14.21 from Bournemouth to Manchester
Piccadilly, where it is due to arrive at 19.31. In
1962, the famous 'Pines Express', routed via the
Somerset & Dorset line, left Bournemouth West
at 9.45am and arrived at Manchester Piccadilly
at 5.2pm. Work out the time difference for
yourself! *Both Author*

256 RINGWOOD

Then : 1958
Ringwood station was situated on the old direct
line, opened in 1847, from Brockenhurst to
Dorchester via Wimborne. On summer
Saturdays in the 1950s and the early 1960s,
some through trains used this route to avoid
congestion in the Bournemouth area. This local
service for Brockenhurst, photographed about
half-a-mile east of the station, consists of 'M7'
0-4-4T No 30028 sandwiched between a
luggage van and a Urie push and pull set.

255 LYMINGTON PIER

Then : 1966

Boats for Yarmouth on the Isle of Wight left from the pier at the end of the 5¼ mile branch from Brockenhurst. On summer Saturdays in the 1950s and early 1960s, through trains to Lymington Pier were worked by 'T9', 'D15' and 'Schools' class 4-4-0 locomotives. M7 0-4-4Ts were used on the local trains to Brockenhurst, but were later replaced by Standard Class 4 2-6-4Ts, such as No 80134 which is about to leave the station.

Now : 9 March 1996

Unfortunately I could not gain access to the position from where the earlier picture was taken, so this view is from the other side of the line. The new terminal building for the Wightlink roll-on roll-off ferry to Yarmouth can be seen in the centre of the picture behind the train. One of the ferry vessels is tied up at the quay to the right of the train. Services on the branch are provided by electric units which shuttle between here and Brockenhurst. One of these trains is arriving at the platform, which gives passengers direct access to the ferry.
Both Author

256 RINGWOOD

Now : 11 March 1996

The line closed to passenger traffic in 1964, and totally in 1977. Since then no effort appears to have been made to claim the trackbed for other use. Amazingly some of the old telegraph poles have survived.
Both Author

257 WIMBORNE

Then : 1960
After leaving Wimborne, the line turned to the south. A Standard Class 4 2-6-0 is crossing the River Stour with a train for Bournemouth West. This particular afternoon must have been warm enough to tempt bathers into the water — the sign on the pontoon in the river reads 'BOATIN AN FISHIN by day or hour NEWMANS BOATS ON THE STOUR'.

Now : 11 March 1996
Though there is now no trace of the railway bridge and the embankment is obscured by trees, boating on the river is as popular as ever. *Both Author*

259 HINTON ADMIRAL

Then : 28 June 1957
The station is on the direct route to Bournemouth via Sway, opened in 1888. On this scorching summer afternoon, 'H15' No 30491 has just stopped at the station with an up local train. No 30491 was originally built by Urie in 1914, but rebuilt by Maunsell in 1927 with a 'King Arthur' type pattern boiler. The locomotive was withdrawn in 1961.

258 BROADSTONE

Then : 1961

At Broadstone, Somerset & Dorset (S&D) line trains branched off the main line to Ringwood. Standard Class 5 4-6-0 No 73049 has just left the station with a local train from the S&D, and is starting the descent of Broadstone's 1 in 75 bank towards Poole. The tracks at the top left of the picture lead to Hamworthy Junction on the line to Wareham and Dorchester.

Now : 11 March 1996

A new recreational centre and swimming pool have made good use of the broad swathe cut by the trackbed of the former lines to Poole and Hamworthy. Though there is now no trace of the railway, the pine trees behind the hut are probably the ones that can just be seen above the footbridge in the earlier picture.
Both Author

259 HINTON ADMIRAL

Now : 9 March 1996

The station, which serves the residential development to the east of Christchurch, has changed very little over the years. An InterCity 125 is passing the station with the 16.16 train from Bournemouth to Manchester Piccadilly.
R. C. Riley/Author

209

260 BOURNEMOUTH CENTRAL/ BOURNEMOUTH (1)

Then : 1964
This is the view from Holdenhurst Road bridge at the eastern end of the station. Rebuilt 'Merchant Navy' No 35007 *Aberdeen Commonwealth* is about to depart with an up express. At this time the two through lines at the station were still in position. However, in connection with the Bournemouth electrification scheme, they were removed, and two sidings created at the west end of the station, as shown in the next pair of pictures.

Now : 9 March 1996
Because of the construction of a garage by the bridge, I had to move rather closer to the line than in the previous picture. Apart from the loss of the two centre lines, referred to above, the station is essentially the same. It is good to see that some attention is being given to the station's rather battered roof. *Both Author*

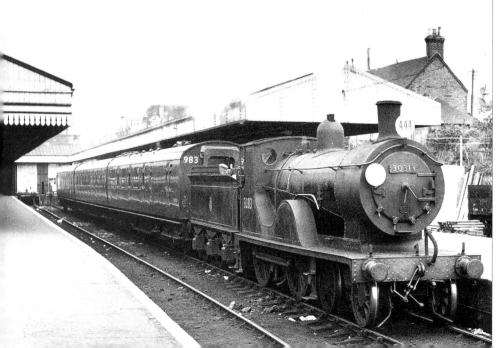

262 BOURNEMOUTH WEST

Then : 1957
The most important trains to use the West station were expresses to Waterloo and those for the Somerset & Dorset line. However, local services to Salisbury and Brockenhurst via Ringwood also began their journeys here, such as this train to Salisbury via Fordingbridge, in charge of 'T9' No 30313.

261 BOURNEMOUTH CENTRAL/ BOURNEMOUTH (2)

Then : 1967

The long down platform gave generations of railway enthusiasts a superb view of the locomotive shed (71B), which closed in July 1967, when full electric services to Waterloo were brought into operation. On the far left is a Class 33 Crompton diesel, a type which for many years, worked push and pull services to Weymouth until that section too was electrified. The steam locomotives visible are Standard Class 5 No 73065, and two Class 4 2-6-0s.

Now : 9 March 1996

The two sidings, used for berthing electric stock, and referred to in the caption for the 1964 picture of Bournemouth, can clearly be seen in this picture. The locomotive shed was quickly demolished at the end of steam, creating the space for a large car park.
Both Author

262 BOURNEMOUTH WEST

Now : 11 March 1996

The short branch from Gas Works Junction, on the main line, to Bournemouth West closed in 1965. The site of the station is now yet another car park, the most tangible link with the past being the buildings in the background. The Midland Hotel, the pointed tower of which is just visible by the side of the canopy on the left hand side of the earlier picture, is particularly distinctive. *Both Author*

263 PARKSTONE

Then : 14 June 1965

Eastbound trains leaving Poole face a stiff climb on a 1 in 60 gradient through Parkstone to Branksome. This picture is taken from the station footbridge which affords a fine view of Poole and this Templecombe to Bournemouth West train in charge of Ivatt 2-6-2T No 41223.

Now : 11 March 1996

The sidings on the left hand side of the picture have been lifted and new building development has taken place by the station. As a change from the usual electric units, a Mainline Class 58 diesel is pounding up the bank with a gas train from Furzebrook. *Derek Cross/Author*

265 CORFE CASTLE

Then : 1962

Services on the Swanage branch were generally in the hands of 'M7' class 0-4-4Ts until their last duty in 1964. Here Nos 30107 and 30108, both fitted for push and pull working, are passing at the fine stone-built station, with trains for Wareham and Swanage respectively.

Now : 10 March 1996

Time seems to have stood still, such is the quality of the restoration work carried out on the station by the Swanage Railway. Originally closed in January 1972, the station was reopened last year as part of the extension to Norden. No 34072 *257 Squadron* is ariving with a train from Swanage. *Both Author*

264 POOLE

Then : 1966

The station is situated on a sharp curve adjacent to Holes Bay, which can just be seen in the background above the train. The driver of No 34098 *Templecombe*, on this service from Weymouth to Bournemouth, must contend with the awkward start from the station and the climb up Parkstone bank which lies ahead.

Now : 11 March 1996

An exact repeat of the earlier picture was not possible since the station has been completely rebuilt. The booking office and other facilities are located on the up side of the line. A link with the past is the block of flats visible above No 34098's train in the 1966 picture.
Both Author

266 HARMAN'S CROSS

Then : 1958

Push and pull fitted No 30111 from Bournemouth shed is propelling its train past Harman's Cross *en route* to Swanage. The Urie push and pull set is strengthened by a compartment coach.

Now : 19 March 1993

Prior to the opening last year of the section of line to Corfe Castle and Norden, Swanage Railway trains terminated at a new station at Harman's Cross. Two unrebuilt Bulleid pacifics, No 34105 *Swanage*, on a visit from the Mid-Hants Railway, and No 34072 *257 Squadron*, make a magnificent sight approaching the station with a special train. This was a recreation of the through trains to Waterloo, which ran from Swanage on summer Saturdays. *Both Author*

267 SWANAGE

Then : 16 October 1965
Ivatt 2-6-2T No 41320 is leaving the station with the 4.5pm train to Wareham. The picture illustrates the goods yard and the general setting of the station in this pleasant resort.

Now : 10 March 1996
Growth of lineside vegetation has prevented me from adopting the same angle as the other picture. However, this view shows some of the developments that have taken place since the Swanage Railway took over. Out of sight to the right of the picture, much of the former goods yard is now occupied by a new supermarket. No 34072 is marshalling its train before leaving for Norden. *M.J.Fox/Author*

Inset : This Wilts & Dorset bus in the yard at Swanage must be the ultimate, and almost convincing, substitute for an engine! *Author*

268 MORETON

Then : 1966
Moreton is a small wayside station situated 6½ miles east of
Dorchester South. Standard Class 5 No 73037 is arriving with a
stopping train for Weymouth.

Now : 11 March 1996
With the removal of the signalbox and the demolition of the station
buildings, the station is now unmanned. A Wessex electric is about to
call at the station to pick up the handful of waiting passengers.
Both Author

269 DORCHESTER SOUTH

Then : May 1953

The railway reached Dorchester from Southampton in 1847, the station building being sited with a view to extending the line westward to Exeter. However, although these plans came to nothing, the original station remained in use to serve trains from Weymouth. A separate platform, from which this picture was taken, was provided for trains to Weymouth. Diesel-electric locomotive No 10000 has come round the curve from Dorchester Junction on the line seen in the left foreground, and run past the station, before backing into the platform. It will then continue the journey eastward to Bournemouth. Nos 10000 and 10001 were on loan from the London Midland Region for some two years from 1953.

Now : 11 March 1996

The new station has been built at a different angle allowing trains from Weymouth a clear run without the need for reversal.
Geoff Rixon/Author

The striking sign for the Station Masters House pub, located near Dorchester South station. *Author*

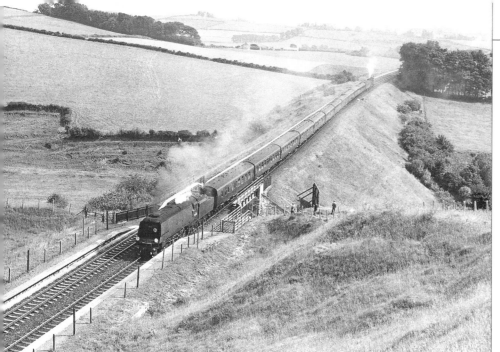

270 UPWEY WISHING WELL HALT

Then : 1965

This diminutive halt, situated to the south of Bincombe tunnel, closed in 1957. Rebuilt 'West Country' pacific No 34041 *Wilton*, is climbing the 1 in 50 gradient past the halt, its train banked at the rear by a Standard Class 5.

Now : 10 March 1996

The platforms of the halt can no longer be seen, but otherwise the location looks essentially unchanged. Due to a serious landslip on the up side of the line south of Bincombe tunnel, all trains were using the down line. This is the 16.30 train from Weymouth to Bristol Temple Meads. *Both Author*

272 WEYMOUTH QUAY

Then : August 1974

In 1959 responsibility for the operation of Channel Island boat trains was transferred from the Western Region to the Southern Region. By the time this picture was taken workings from the Quay were in the hands of Class 33 Crompton diesels. The slow progress of the boat trains along the quay was always something of an event, especially when cars had to be manhandled off the tracks.

This Waterloo bound train is preceded by two railway employees who will ensure that the route ahead is clear. Note the small bell fitted on the front of the diesel.

271 WEYMOUTH

Then : 1964
LSWR trains reached Weymouth under the terms of an agreement on joint use of the line from Dorchester Junction. Some of the old wooden platforms still survive in this view showing Standard Class 4 No 76010 arriving with a down stopping train. The line to Weymouth Quay diverges from the main line just out of sight on the left hand side of this picture.

Now : 10 March 1996
I have had to stand in a slightly different position from the earlier picture as the once extensive railway infrastructure at Weymouth has dramatically contracted. A Wessex electric is arriving with a train from Bournemouth. *Both Author*

272 WEYMOUTH QUAY

Now : 11 March 1996
Although the track is still in place and well polished by the movement of traffic, there are no longer any boat trains. *Both Author*

273 WHITCHURCH

Then : 1959
Rebuilt 'Merchant Navy' No 35030 *Elder Dempster Lines* is speeding through the station with the down 'Atlantic Coast Express', first stop Salisbury. Just visible on the extreme left of the picture is the bay platform once used by trains on the line to Fullerton Junction via Hurstbourne, which was closed to passengers in 1931.

Now : 3 April 1996
Apart from new station furniture, the most noticeable change is the raising of the platforms to accommodate modern trains. A Class 159 unit is bringing commuters back from London on the 17.59 arrival.

274 ANDOVER JUNCTION/ANDOVER

Then : August 1967

A sad picture showing the departure of rebuilt 'Merchant Navy' pacifics Nos 35023 and 35008 to Salisbury for storage prior to dispatch to South Wales for cutting up. Crompton diesel No D6549 is working hard to get its load moving up the long climb to Grateley.

Now : 3 April 1996

There has been much simplification of the track layout since the previous picture was taken almost 30 years ago. On the left of the picture are the sidings used by military traffic to the MoD depot at Ludgershall, on the old Midland & South Western Junction line to Cheltenham. A Class 159 unit, used on Waterloo to Exeter line services, is leaving the station with the 17.14 train to Salisbury. *John Bird/Author*

275 ANDOVER TOWN

Then : 1957

Andover Town station on the line to Fullerton Junction and Romsey was closed to passengers in 1964. Prior to the introduction of Hampshire diesel multiple-units on services in the area, the 'T9' class enjoyed an Indian Summer on these trains. No 30284, from Eastleigh shed, is entering the station with a train for its home town.

Now : 3 April 1996

Such has been the extent of road and building development that it is very difficult to believe trains once passed this spot. However, amazingly some of the station's concrete platform fencing still remains in the hedge to the left of this picture. The other point of reference is the church tower, which, in the earlier picture, can be seen above the second coach of the train. *Both Author*

276 HORSEBRIDGE

Then : 1957
Another train from Andover Junction to Eastleigh is pulling out of the station behind 'T9' class 4-4-0 No 30726, with a set of one of Bullied's earlier design of main line coaches painted in carmine and cream. The LSWR signalbox and lower quadrant signal complete this pleasant scene.

Now : 3 April 1996
The owners of the station have undertaken a great deal of work to preserve the platform and buildings, though the signal and signalbox are not original. The vehicle in the southbound platform is an example of a LSWR Ironclad coach designed by Robert Urie. *Both Author*

278 NEWTON TONY

Then : 14 May 1955
This obscure station was on the line to Bulford was built primarily to serve the Army camps in the area. It closed to passenger traffic in 1952, by which time the service had been reduced to just one train in each direction between Salisbury and Bulford on Monday to Saturday. The train in this picture is a Railway Enthusiasts Club railtour from Andover hauled by one of the Beattie Well Tanks, No 30587, which was normally based at Wadebridge in Cornwall (see pages xxx and xxx Boscarne and Wenford Bridge).

277 MOTTISFONT

Then : 5 October 1957
The 1.42pm Andover to Portsmouth train, hauled by 'T9' class 4-4-0 No 30288, will soon be joining the line from Salisbury at Kimbridge Junction, a short distance south of the station.

Now : 3 April 1996
The attractive hung tiled station has now been converted to a private residence offering no clues that the railway once crossed the road at this point. *Colin Hogg/Author*

278 NEWTON TONY

Now : 3 April 1996
The site of the station has been cleared though the odd concrete post survives. The trackbed in the direction of Amesbury and Bulford can, however, be clearly seen. *Colin Hogg/Author*

279 SALISBURY

Then : 23 March 1963
This view of the west end of the station shows a freight train for the Exeter line hauled by Urie 'S15' No 30496. The old Great Western Railway station was located behind No 1 platform, which can be seen on the far left of the picture. On the right is No 5 platform used by local trains to the West of England line.

Now : 13 March 1996
Whilst the station itself remains remarkably unchanged, a maintenance depot for the Class 159 diesel units used on the West of England line has been built on the area once occupied by the old GWR. No 5, the down side bay platform, is still in use, though the adjacent goods yard is now a car park. A Class 158 unit is leaving on a service to Cardiff.
J. N. Faulkner/Author

280 TEMPLECOMBE

Then : 18 July 1953

A scene so evocative of the early 1950s when Templecombe was a busy interchange point for trains to Exeter, Salisbury and over the Somerset & Dorset route. This picture is taken at the west end of the station looking towards Sherborne. To the left of that wonderful nameboard is H15 No 30334 waiting to work a passenger train to Salisbury (see also the picture of this locomotive at Surbiton on page 159), as well as a Somerset & Dorset 2-8-0 on freight duty in the extensive goods yard.

Now : 13 March 1996

Templecombe was one of seven intermediate stations between Salisbury and Exeter that closed from 7 March 1966. However, thanks to a joint initiative between British Rail, the Somerset County Council and local people, a new station was opened on 3 October 1983. I have had to take this picture from a slightly different angle because of the position of the new boundary fence. The up line platform seen in the previous picture is however, clearly visible, behind which is the overgrown site of the freight yard. *Geoff Rixon/Author*

The new station looking west showing the 16.20 train from Exeter St David's. The only clear link with the old station is the signal box. *Author*

281 YEOVIL JUNCTION

Then : 8 September 1962

The station is situated almost two miles from Yeovil itself. A push and pull train, worked by an 'M7' 0-4-4T in later years, provided a connection to Yeovil Town station. Unrebuilt 'West Country' pacific No 34091 *Weymouth* is about to depart with the 9am train from Waterloo to Exeter Central. The photographer records that this locomotive had replaced 'Merchant Navy' No 35018 which had failed at Basingstoke.

Now : 13 March 1996

Now that the down platforms have been taken out of use, the covered footbridge has suffered some drastic 'pruning' giving the structure an oddly unbalanced appearance. Because the line to Yeovil Town has been closed, a bus link provides transport into the town.
L. Sandler/Author

282 YEOVIL TOWN

Then : 8 September 1961
Opened in 1861, the joint GWR/LSWR station was closed to passengers in October 1966. This interesting view looking towards Yeovil Junction shows, from left to right: a Western Region train from Pen Mill about to depart for Taunton, a through train from Yeovil Town to Exeter Central, the Yeovil Town to Yeovil Junction push and pull shuttle, and the locomotive shed (72C).

Now : 13 March 1996
The view today is uninteresting in the extreme, for the whole area is now a large car park. The bridge in the background which was partially obscured by the station footbridge in the 1961 picture, carries the road leading to Yeovil Junction. *R. N. Joanes/Author*

283 AXMINSTER

Then : 1952

Axminster was the junction for the winding 6¼ mile long branch to Lyme Regis, which opened in 1903. The bay for the branch was situated alongside the up main line platform, where unrebuilt 'Merchant Navy' pacific No 35003 *Royal Mail* has stopped with an express from Exeter to Waterloo. The locomotive will now face a climb of 10 miles or so up the valley of the River Axe to Hewish.

Now : 29 March 1996

The site of the up bay platform used by Lyme Regis trains, which were withdrawn on 29 November 1965, is visible on the right hand side of the picture. The main line has now been singled, thus isolating the one-time up platform. A Class 159 unit is calling at the neat and well kept station before continuing its journey east. The loss of the glazed footbridge has to some extent been compensated for by the decorative new platform canopy. I have had to take this view further forward because there was a barrier restricting access under the bridge.

F. R. Hebron(Rail Archive Stephenson)/Author

284 LYME REGIS

Then : undated but mid-1950s

Lyme Regis station, like Ventnor in the Isle of Wight, was situated high above the town centre. This is the classic view of the station from the buffer stops, and shows Adams Radial tank No 30582 not long after arrival with a train from Axminster. These locomotives worked trains on the branch until they were replaced by Ivatt 2-6-2Ts in 1961. After closure a section of the station buildings from Lyme Regis was rescued and is now used as the buffet at Alresford station on the Mid-Hants Railway.

Now : 29 March 1996

The site of the station is now a small industrial estate, the only traces of its former life being some railway concrete posts on the boundary of the site. The tree-line in the background of both pictures is the only feature which helps to link the two. *J. Davenport/Author*

285 SEATON JUNCTION

Then : 23 September 1959

A fine view of the station looking west, showing rebuilt 'Merchant Navy' No 35003 *Royal Mail* on an up express for Waterloo. In the westbound direction trains face a long climb up Honiton bank which is on a gradient of 1 in 80 for most of its length. Because visibility was limited on the curved approach to the station from the west, the starting signal is fitted with repeater arms. The signals controlling the Seaton branch are on the far left of the picture.

Now : 29 March 1996

With the closure of the Seaton branch, the station lost the principal reason for its existence, since there were no settlements of any size nearby. A Class 159 unit on the 13.30 train from Exeter St David's is sweeping through the remains of the station. The footbridge nearest to the camera gave access to the down and Seaton branch platforms, whilst the further one still carries a public footpath.
K. L. Cook (Rail Archive Stephenson)/Author

287 SEATON

Then : 1962

Holiday-makers' enjoying a visit to the cab of 'M7' No 30667 or looking at the engine, create a happy picture at the terminus, which was rebuilt in the mid-1930s. The roof of the small single-road engine shed can be seen above the cab of the engine.

286 COLYTON

Then : 1958

Colyton was the first station from Seaton Junction on the 4½ mile long branch to Seaton, which lost its service in 1966. 'M7' 0-4-4Ts worked on the line for many years, until their last duties in 1963. In this picture, 'M7' No 30021, fitted with push and pull gear, is about to propel its two-coach Urie set out of the station for Colyford and Seaton.

Now : 29 March 1996

The station is now the northern terminus of the Seaton Tramway which opened in 1980. Apart from a loop to its southern terminus at Seaton, the tramway runs along the trackbed of the old branch. This picture shows the considerable amount of work being undertaken at the station in preparation for the forthcoming season. *Both Author*

287 SEATON

Now : 29 March 1996

The site of the station is now occupied by Racal, the well known electronics firm. The windows of the house across the road from the terminus can be seen in both pictures. *Both Author*

288 SIDMOUTH JUNCTION/FENITON

Then : August 1963

Sidmouth Junction was the starting point of the branches to Sidmouth and Exmouth via Tipton St John's, which closed to passenger traffic in 1967. Originally named Feniton after the village in which it was situated, the station took this name again when it was reopened in 1971. No 41307 and a Standard 2-6-4T are waiting to leave the down main line platform with through coaches for Tipton St John's and Exmouth. Some of the houses in the village of Feniton can be seen to the right of the engine.

Now : 29 March 1996

New housing development in the village, was the primary reason for reopening the station. Although it is not visible in this photograph, a new but modest station office has been built on the one-time down side of the line. This combines the functions of booking office and level crossing control cabin for the road which crosses the line at this point. Unit No 159011 is speeding through the station with the 15.45 train from Exeter St David's to Waterloo.
J. N. Faulkner/Author

289 TIPTON ST JOHN'S

Then : 22 August 1958
Tipton St John's was the junction for the lines to Sidmouth and Exmouth, which in the down direction were controlled by the fine LSWR lower quadrant signal at the end of the platform. Beyond the footbridge and level crossing, the line to Sidmouth can be seen receding into the distance. Standard Class 3 2-6-2T No 82019, one of a batch built at Swindon for the Southern Region, has arrived with a train from the Sidmouth line.

Now : 29 March 1996
The former buildings on the up platform at this once busy station are now a pleasant private residence. This faces on to a wide grassed area once occupied by the trackbed and the down platform. The chimney pots on the platform in front of the telephone kiosk were saved from the original station chimneys when they were taken down. *J. N. Faulkner/Author*

290 SIDMOUTH

Then : August 1953
'M7' No 30670 is waiting to leave the station with a train for Sidmouth Junction. The station, which was situated a little distance north of the town centre, consisted of an island platform, flanked by engine and goods sheds.

Now : 29 March 1996
The station building is well preserved, and the platform area is now used by a garage. It is pleasing to see that the roof and canopy have been retained though the site is rather cramped. The remainder of the site is used for small offices and light industry, but the new development has made it impossible to repeat exactly the earlier view. *Ian Allan Library/Author*

291 BUDLEIGH SALTERTON

Then : 17 August 1963

No 82001 is arriving with a train for Exmouth. Beyond the footbridge is the small road bridge which offered a good overall view of the station.

Now : 29 March 1996

New housing development now occupies the point where the previous picture was taken, so I have had to move back to present a more general view. This picture is taken from a supermarket car park which occupies the trackbed and former goods yard to the west of the station. *J. N. Faulkner/Author*

293 EXETER CENTRAL (1)

Then : 26 May 1958

Howell Road bridge provides an excellent viewpoint for this picture of 'M7' No 30023, which has been smartly turned out by Exmouth Junction shed. The locomotive is pulling out of the up bay platform with a train for Exmouth, consisting of British Railways standard suburban stock. Exeter Central A box dominates the view behind the locomotive.

292 EXMOUTH

Then : 13 October 1959
A fine overall view of the station showing 'M7' 0-4-4T No 30676 reversing a train into the platform prior to departure for Tipton St John's. The small engine shed can be seen above the van of No 30676's train. On the far right hand side, a service for Exeter Central is waiting to leave hauled by a Standard Class 3 2-6-2T.

Now : 30 March 1996
This once extensive station has been reduced to a single platform, flanked on one side by a new relief road from the dock area. On the other side there is an extensive car and coach park bordering on the River Exe. The church spire and the line of buildings behind the station are the most obvious link with the previous photograph. *R. C. Riley/Author*

293 EXETER CENTRAL (1)

Now : 30 March 1996
The reduction in facilities at Exeter Central is all too apparant in this picture. Unit No 159001 is leaving the station with the 11.35 train from Exeter St David's to Waterloo. The signalbox closed in the mid-1980s, but continues to be a reminder of the busy service that once used the main line to Salisbury, prior to the run down of this route in the late 1960s. *John P. Wilson (Rail Archive Stephenson)/Author*

294 EXETER CENTRAL (2)

Then : 29 May 1950

Exeter Central was known as Exeter Queen Street until it was given its present name in 1933. This picture is taken from the bridge which carries Queen Street itself over the railway at the west end of the station. Unrebuilt 'West Country' No 34024 *Tamar Valley* is nearing the end of the 1 in 37 bank which brings the line up from Exeter St David's. In the small yard on the other side of the line to the carriage sidings, one of the 'E1/R' 0-6-2Ts, No 32124, employed to bank trains up the gradient, is on station pilot duties.

Now : 30 March 1996

Car parking and temporary office accommodation now occupy the sites of the former yards. A Class 150 Sprinter unit is coming up the bank with the 11.51 service from St David's to Exmouth. The course of the old up line trap siding, which has been replaced by catch points, can be seen behind the front of the train.

John P. Wilson (Rail Archive Stephenson)/Author

296 NEWTON ST CYRES

Then : 1958

This small station is situated in the valley of the River Creedy by the village of Sweetham. Newton St Cyres itself lies almost a mile to the south. Unrebuilt 'West Country' No 34108 *Wincanton* is coasting through the station with a train from Ilfracombe. No 34108 was rebuilt in 1961 and was destined to last until June 1967, just before the end of steam on the Southern.

The station nameboard. With the onset of railway privatisation, it is to be hoped that the BR logo will be retained in all parts of the country as a universally recognisable station sign. *Author*

295 COWLEY BRIDGE JUNCTION

Then : Summer 1957
The Southern line to the west and the Western Region line to Taunton, diverged at Cowley Bridge. Heading a train from Ilfracombe and Barnstaple, 'N' class No 31838 is coasting over the junction, and past its controlling signalbox, to join the WR route.

Now : 30 March 1996
A considerable amount of civil engineering work has been undertaken at the junction since 1957, including the singling of the track on the Southern route. In conjunction with flood protection work, the course of the River Exe has been altered, necessitating the construction of a new bridge and the removal of the old one by the junction. Unit No 150249 is working the 12.35 train from Crediton to Exmouth.
Colin Hogg/Author

296 NEWTON ST CYRES

Now : 30 March 1996
Although the down line has been removed, the remains of its platform is still visible. Only a very limited number of trains stop at this now unstaffed station. *Both Author*

297 CREDITON

Then : 1957
The station was opened in 1851 as part of the Bristol & Exeter Railway Co line from Exeter. 'N' class No 31832 is passing the well preserved buildings with a train from Padstow and Okehampton.

Now : 30 March 1996
If anything the station looks better cared for than it did in the 1950s. Few changes have taken place, other than the reduction of the buildings on the down side and the removal of the covering to the footbridge in the background. On the down side of the station there is a large park and ride car park facility for passengers visiting Exeter. *Both Author*

298 LAPFORD

Then : undated but circa early 1960s

Lapford is a small station situated in the valley of the River Yeo, which the Barnstaple to Exeter line follows at this point. The station was unusual in that the up and down platforms were separated by the A377 road which crosses the line at this point. Unrebuilt Bulleid pacific No 34066 *Spitfire* is entering the station with a train from Ilfracombe.

Now : 24 August 1993

This picture was taken from the A377 road bridge, to show the whole of the well kept station building. The down platform, on the other side of the bridge behind the photographer, was demolished in the early 1970s, so a single line now leads through the station. *Lens of Sutton/ Terry Gough*

299 BARNSTAPLE JUNCTION

Then : 20 July 1964

The station looking north west towards the junction of the lines from Ilfracombe and Torrington. A train for Barnstaple Victoria Road station and Taunton is waiting in the long platform. The goods yard and locomotive shed (72E) were located out of sight to the right of the picture.

Now : 2 April 1996

The extent of the contraction of the facilities at the station is starkly visible in this present day view. The two-coach Sprinter unit, forming the 14.23 service to Exmouth, is almost lost to view amidst the barren platforms. Even the canopy on the surviving platform has been cut back. An office at the station hires bicycles out for use on the Tarka Trail which runs along the trackbed of the former line towards Torrington, closed to passengers in 1965. *R. C. Riley/Author*

300 BARNSTAPLE RIVER TAW BRIDGE

Then : 19 May 1959
A classic view across the River Taw from the west bank. Unrebuilt Bulleid pacific No 34063 *229 Squadron* has just left the Town station, and is crossing the 213yd long bridge across the river. The train is the 2.20pm from Ilfracombe to Waterloo where it is due at 8.25pm. The line to Ilfracombe closed to passengers in 1970.

Now : 2 April 1996
The view across the river is tranquil, the smooth water giving no hint that such a large structure crossed it at this point. The line of buildings on the opposite bank is unchanged, though the Regal cinema no longer advertises it presence.
K. L. Cook (Rail Archive Stephenson)/Author

302 WOODY BAY

Then : undated but probably early 1930s
The approach to the station from the west, with a train arriving for Lynton on its 19½ mile journey from Barnstaple. This picture gives some idea of the beautiful high country the railway ran through. In the background are the hills facing on to the Bristol Channel east of Ilfracombe. The line was closed by the Southern Railway for economy reasons in 1935, an act that future generations have never forgiven. Had the railway survived it would surely have equalled the splendours of the Ffestiniog Railway in North Wales.

301 CHELFHAM VIADUCT

Then : undated but probably c1900
The greatly mourned 1ft 11½ in gauge Lynton and Barnstaple line wound up the lovely valley of the River Yeo, before turning eastward on to the slopes of Exmoor. The viaduct crossed a valley cut by a tributary of the Yeo at Chelfham. This picture was taken from the hillside to the northeast of the viaduct. Such is the pristine condition of the structure, that the picture probably dates from not long after the line opened in 1898.

Now : 2 April 1996
When driving through this area, the sudden appearance of this impressive curved viaduct never fails to surprise the traveller. The years have treated the viaduct fairly kindly, though the buildings below the arches, detract from its impact. Because of the growth of woodland on the hillside, I have had to take this wide-angle-lens picture from the road.
Courtesy Knights Photographers Barnstaple/Author

A close up of the arches from the west side.
Author

302 WOODY BAY

Now : 2 April 1996
The landscape looks much the same on this still, quiet evening as it did all those years ago. To the left some of the old railway buildings, dating back to the early 1900s, still survive. There are plans to relay a stretch of the trackbed from Woody Bay and operate passenger trains. It is to be hoped that the scheme will not destroy the fragile beauty of this place.
Courtesy Knights Photographers Barnstaple/Author

303 MORTEHOE & WOOLACOMBE

Then : 14 September 1963

The station was set some 600ft up about two miles from the villages of Mortehoe and Woolacombe. The railway timetable shows a note to the effect that it was also the station for Lee, three miles distant. No 34065 *Hurricane* has arrived at the station with the 4.50pm train from Ilfracombe to Exeter Central. The train will have been allowed about 12 minutes to cover the 3½ miles up the 1 in 36 bank from Ilfracombe, an average speed of around 17 mph!

Now : 2 April 1996

Most of the station site has been transformed to become the 'Once Upon A Time' childrens' adventure playground. Ironically a miniature play railway now occupies part of the trackbed — the train of 'engines' can be seen on the left of the picture. *J. Scrace/Author*

305 OKEHAMPTON

Then : c1957

A pleasing scene at the station as many like to remember it. 'T9' class 4-4-0 No 30717, with a train from Plymouth, is running in to the up platform, where passengers are ready to board and put their bicycles in the guard's van. At the end of the down platform the signal, with its repeater arm, is 'off' for a westbound train. This will face a steep climb out of the station towards Meldon.

304 ILFRACOMBE

Then : 18 May 1959

A splendid view of the shed and station set high above the town. 'N' class 2-6-0 No 31835 is on shed — it has probably just been on the 70ft turntable, the railings of which can just be seen in the foreground of the picture. The carriage sidings at the side of the station are extensive enough to berth all the rakes of stock required during the busy holiday season.

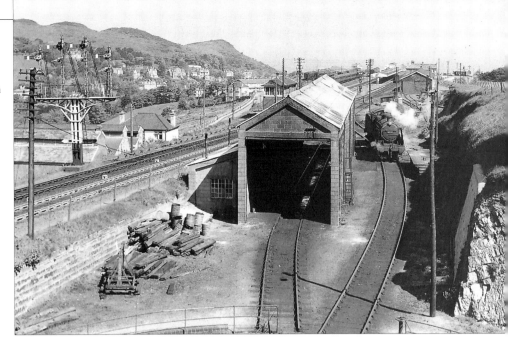

Now : 2 April 1996

The site of the station is now occupied by a factory and office development. A path can be followed to the point where the earlier picture was taken, although I have had to stand a little further forward to avoid the view being blocked by trees in the wood behind me. Removal of the railway and subsequent land infill has drastically altered the appearance of the site.
K. L. Cook (Rail Archive Stephenson)/Author

305 OKEHAMPTON

Now : 30 March 1996

On this warm sunny afternoon the station stands silent, and stripped of all its fittings. The line to Okehampton lost its regular passenger service from Exeter in June 1972. It is now only used by ballast trains to and from Meldon Quarry some two miles to the west. Whether the route will ever reopen to passenger traffic remains to be seen, but the inconvenient location of Okehampton station high above the centre of the town, is a disadvantage.
Colin Hogg/Author

306 MELDON VIADUCT

Then : undated but c1958
The 120ft high viaduct carries the line over the ravine cut by the West Okement river. This view is taken looking west towards Meldon Junction where the lines to Plymouth and Halwill diverged. 'T9' 4-4-0 No 30726 is on a train from Plymouth. The engine finished its days working from Exmouth Junction shed, and was withdrawn from service in August 1959.

Now : 30 March 1996
The viaduct seen from a slightly lower and more broadside position, to avoid the scrub which now obscures the structure from some angles. This listed structure is now completely closed and fenced off to prevent trespass by the public. *S. C. Nash/Author*

The view across the viaduct from Meldon Quarry. In the background South Down, 1,227ft high, marks the beginning of Dartmoor. *Author*

308 HATHERLEIGH

Then : 7 September 1960
The North Devon & Cornwall Junction Light Railway ran for 20½ miles between Torrington and Halwill Junction. The line was engineered by Colonel Stephens, who had also been involved in the construction of a number of other light railways, such as the Hawkhurst branch in Kent. Partially built on the route of an earlier narrow gauge railway, the line opened on 27 July 1925. Because of the remote country through which it ran, passenger expectations could never have been very high. The most important traffic was china clay, principally from the workings between Petrockstow and Meeth. At Hatherleigh station, which was situated some distance from the town, Ivatt 2-6-2T No 41295 is about to leave with the 4pm train from Torrington to Halwill.

307 HALWILL JUNCTION

Then : 3 September 1954

Halwill was the junction for the lines to Padstow (the North Cornwall line), Bude and Torrington. 'T9' No 30710, with a train for Padstow, is blowing off vigorously before departing for Ashwater, five miles further on. Halwill Junction also served the village of Beaworthy about a mile to the east. The station buildings are just to the right of the lattice signal post.

Now : 1 April 1996

The site of the station is now a large housing estate. After some deliberation I decided that if I was to stand in the same place as the earlier view, the result would be a picture of a brick wall. I have therefore moved slightly further forward and to the left, to show the Junction Inn. This building can be seen on the left hand side in both pictures. *J. N. Faulkner/Author*

308 HATHERLEIGH

Now : 1 April 1996

The station has now been incorporated into a private residence. This view, taken from the overgrown trackbed to the south of the station, shows the post of the down starting signal. *E. T. Gill/Author*

309 PETROCKSTOW

Then : 7 November 1959
Petrockstow was located just over half way between Halwill and Torrington. The goods yard was on the northbound side of the line, and can be seen on the left of this picture. A train for Torrington is waiting to leave the station. By the early 1960s there were only two through trains per day in each direction, which were allowed almost an hour and a half for the journey! The line closed to passengers at the beginning of March 1965, though the clay traffic lasted for another 17 years.

Now : 3 May 1993
The remains of the platform can still be clearly be seen. Much of the trackbed of the line now forms the Tarka Trail for walkers and cyclists. Incidentally on the Ordnance Survey map, Petrockstow is spelt with an 'e' at the end of the word, though the BR timetable shows it without this final letter. *Chris Gammell/ Terry Gough*

311 WHITSTONE & BRIDGERULE

Then : 1963
One of the BR Class 3 2-6-2Ts allocated to Exmouth Junction, is waiting to leave the neatly kept station with a train from Bude to Halwill. The station was about a mile to the south of the village of Bridgerule, and some two miles north of Whitstone, so was poorly sited for both communities. Note the old style station nameboard on the left hand side of the picture.

310 TORRINGTON

Then : undated but early 1960s

Torrington was at the end of the 14¾ mile long line from Barnstaple Junction, from which Ivatt 2-6-2T No 41310 has just arrived. These locomotives replaced the Drummond 'M7' 0-4-4Ts on local services from Barnstaple. Torrington enjoyed a through service to and from Waterloo — for example in the summer of 1952, coaches leaving Torrington at 8.10am were scheduled to arrive at Waterloo at 2.1pm. Behind the train are some milk tankers for the creamery by the station.

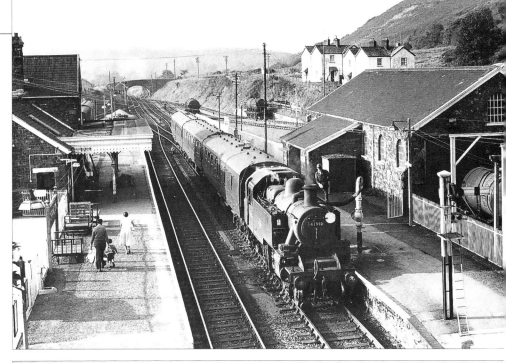

Now : 2 April 1996

Although the trains have gone, the site is well cared for. The station has now been converted to a public house called the Puffing Billy. The siding and goods wagon that have recently been installed provide a link with the past. The Tarka Trail can be seen stretching away into the distance. It continues in the other direction across the viaduct over the River Torridge, on the trackbed of the old line to Halwill.
Terry Gough/Author

311 WHITSTONE & BRIDGERULE

Now : 1 April 1996

The station, which is now a private residence, is remarkably complete on the down side as the picture shows, though the space between the platforms has been filled in. The bridge in the background carries the B3254 road over the line. *Both Author*

312 BUDE

Then : 1960

The station was situated on the southwestern edge of the town. It consisted of a main platform, long enough to handle holiday trains, and a shorter bay. On this sunny afternoon, 'N' class 2-6-0 No 31836 is in the bay platform with a train for Halwill. Like Torrington, Bude enjoyed a through service to and from Waterloo, including a portion on the fabled 'Atlantic Coast Express'. Sadly the line did not survive the Beeching cuts and was closed in October 1966.

Now : 1 April 1996

It is impossible to believe that the station was ever here. Although they are obscured from where I am standing, reference to the houses on the skyline behind the 'N' class in the earlier picture, helped pinpoint the position. The new development on the site of the station consists of sheltered housing for the elderly.

Terry Gough/Author

314 GUNNISLAKE

Then : 25 June 1959

The station was set on a hillside southwest of the village which borders the River Tamar. Ivatt 2-6-2T No 41317 has arrived at the station with a mixed freight train, prior to shunting in the yard.

313 BERE ALSTON

Then : 1958

Bere Alston, on the main Okehampton to Plymouth line, was the junction for the 9½ miles long Plymouth Devonport and South Western Junction Railway to Callington, opened in 1908. Trains for the branch left from the outer face of the island platform on the up side of the line. The Adams O2 class 0-4-4Ts were the usual motive power for passenger trains in the 1950s. On this warm summer morning, one of these locomotives, No 30225, is waiting to leave for Callington, whilst the train crew chat on the platform.

Now : 1 April 1996

The station is now reduced to a single line running in to the former down main line platform, just out of sight on the right of the picture. The former signal box and waiting shelter survive on the old up platform. Trains from Plymouth to Gunnislake reverse at the station to gain access to the branch. The points for the line leading to it, are controlled from a ground frame at the end of the station platform. North of the Bere Alston station, the track is lifted all the way to Meldon Quarry (see page 242). *Both Author*

314 GUNNISLAKE

Now : 1 April 1996

The station has now been closed, and a new one opened on the other side of the A390 road, which used to go under the line at the Calstock end of the station. The site of the old station was advertised for sale at the time of my visit. Only the island platform remains, the near face of which can be seen in both pictures. Because of the growth of trees and scrub on the site, this is the nearest I could get to the 1959 picture. *Antony Linaker/Author*

The new station at Gunnislake, which was opened in June 1994. The old station was located on the other side of the road beyond the buffer stops. *Author*

247

315 LUCKETT

Then : 1957

Luckett station was situated on the northeast side of the 1,092ft high Kit Hill, which dominates the view around Callington. An 'O2' 0-4-4T is arriving at the single platform with a train from Callington to Bere Alston. Note the two neat rows of hanging fire buckets under the station nameboard and the selection of luggage barrows on the platform. Would traffic levels at this small station have ever warranted use of so many barrows I wonder?

Now : 1 April 1996

The platform is still clearly visible, but otherwise there are no other traces of the station. *Both Author*

316 CALLINGTON

Then : 1958

Callington station was situated in the village of Kelly Bray about a mile north of Callington itself. The old chimney of a mine on Kit Hill stands out on the skyline behind the small locomotive shed in the station yard. 'O2' 0-4-4T No 30225 is running round its train before returning to Bere Alston. Passenger traffic on the line beyond Gunnislake was never heavy, so unfortunately this section of the line closed in November 1966.

Now : 1 April 1996

The site of the station is now an industrial estate. The chimneys of the cottage in the background, can just be seen above the white building in front of the 'O2' in the earlier picture. *Both Author*

317 ST BUDEAUX VICTORIA ROAD

Then : April 1951

The station was situated to the north of Devonport. Many of those employed in the nearby dockyard would have lived in the network of streets surrounding Victoria Road station. Unrebuilt 'West Country' Pacific No 34036 *Westward Ho*, which entered traffic in July 1946, is drawing to a halt at the station with a train from Exeter.

Now : 1 April 1996

The once well equipped station has now been reduced to a single platform with a bus stop type shelter, and is only used by trains to Bere Alston and Gunnislake. This is the 09.30 train from Plymouth to Gunnislake which gained one passenger at the station. *W. J. Verden Anderson (Rail Archive Stephenson)/Author*

318 PLYMOUTH FRIARY

Then : 15 April 1956
The bridge spanning the lines to the east of Friary station can just be seen in this picture of unrebuilt 'West Country' pacific No 34034 *Honiton* shortly after leaving the terminus. The train will soon pass the Southern's Plymouth Friary locomotive shed (72D).

Now : 31 March 1996
The station closed to passengers in 1958 to became a freight depot, but the site has since been sold for building development. The rusty lines now stop this side of the road bridge at the end of the station.
Terry Gough/Author

319 LAUNCESTON

Then : 1958
The Great Western station was located behind this train from Plymouth and Tavistock, which is hauled by '4500' class 2-6-2T No 5531 from Laira shed, Plymouth. The Western station closed in 1952 to become a goods depot, so by the time this picture was taken, both North Cornwall line and Plymouth trains used the Southern station.

Now : 30 March 1996
Nothing remains of the two stations at Launceston, which have become the site of a large industrial estate. The lone Great Western Railway signal serves to advertise that steam trains can still be seen on the nearby Launceston Steam Railway. Its new station is located on the west side of the bridge that carries the A388 road over the railway. The new narrow gauge line runs for some two miles along along the trackbed of the old North Cornwall line towards Egloskerry.
Both Author

One of the Launceston Steam Railway locomotives — note the nameboard from the Southern station, which may well be the one visible behind No 5531 in the 1958 picture.
Author

320 OTTERHAM

Then : August 1964
Otterham station, on the North Cornwall line, was set near the summit of the line high above the village. A Standard 2-6-4T has paused at the station with a local train from Padstow to Okehampton. The bridge in the background carried the A39 road over the line. Note the solid stone-built shelter on the down platform. A shelter built to the same design still exists at St Kew Highway (see page 253).

Now : 1 April 1996
Fortunately the station house has survived, and the present owner has plans to restore as many of the old railway features as possible. The bridge that carried the A39 road over the line has been demolished and the trackbed filled in.
Andrew Muckley/Author

321 CAMELFORD

Then : July 1960

The station was situated in an exposed position well out of the town, so the name 'Camelford Road' might have been more appropriate. In the latter years of steam, local trains were worked by Exmouth Junction's stud of 'N' class 2-6-0s, which were ideally suited to the sharp curves and steep gradients on the line. One of these locomotives, No 31834, is calling at the station with a eastbound train. It is carrying two oil lamps either side of the smokebox instead of the white disc route codes, so this picture may have been taken close to dusk.

Now : 1 April 1996

The station is now the Museum of Historic Cycling. I have taken the picture from a slightly wider angle to show more of the museum and station building. The visitor can see a length of the original platforms on the other side of the building in the centre of the picture.
David Lawrence/Author

323 WADEBRIDGE

Then : 1958

The Padstow end of the station showing Beattie 2-4-0 Well Tank station pilot No 30586, shunting some wagons. To the right of the coal stack is the shed turntable. Beyond it, is what looks like a South Eastern & Chatham Railway Birdcage coach — if so it is very far from home. Perhaps it was used as a mess vehicle?

322 ST KEW HIGHWAY

Then : 1958
On this sunny evening two trains are crossing at the station. The westbound service for Padstow is headed by unrebuilt 'West Country' No 34029 *Lundy*. Through the windows of his box, the signalman can be seen operating the signal levers ready for the departure of the two trains. Apart from when it passed through stations, the North Cornwall line was single line throughout from Meldon Junction to Padstow.

Now : 31 March 1996
A photograph from the same position as the earlier picture would only have shown the back wall of a barn, so I have moved to the other side of it. The gate in this view can just be seen on the extreme left hand side of the earlier picture, and beyond that the edge of the station house. Just visible in the middle distance, is the gable end of the former down platform waiting shelter. *Both Author*

323 WADEBRIDGE

Now : 31 March 1996
Returning to Wadebridge for the first time in some 34 years, I felt like a time traveller from another age, so complete has been the elimination of the railway. However, part of the station buildings survive as the John Betjeman Centre. In this view all traces of the railway have gone, although the buildings in the background have hardly changed. *Both Author*

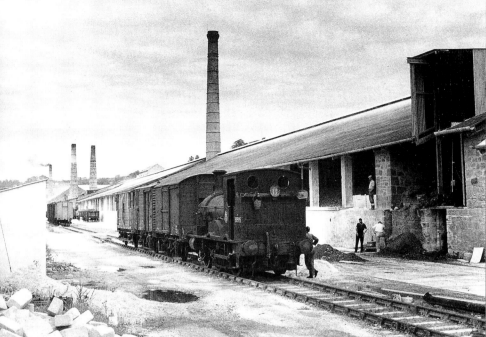

324 WENFORD BRIDGE CLAY WORKS

Then : 1959

The china clay works was situated some six miles from Boscarne Junction. The line ran up the beautiful wooded valley of the River Camel. This provided a superb setting in which to photograph the Beattie Well tanks used on the clay trains for many years until 1962. No 30585 has finished its shunting at the works, and is ready for the return journey to Wadebridge.

Now : 31 March 1996

The line closed in 1983, and nowadays the clay is carried by lorry through the narrow, winding and sometimes very steep lanes. Whether a scheme to reopen the line to rail traffic will succeed remains to be seen. In the meantime, apart from the loss of the rails and alterations to the chimneys, the scene at the works is not that different. The light on the shed to the left is a reminder of the security problems of modern times. *Both Author*

The Camel Trail information board in the car park at Poley's Bridge by the clay works. The trail runs to Wadebridge and Padstow. *Author*

325 BODMIN NORTH

Then : 1960

Adams 'O2' class 0-4-4T No 30199 is waiting to leave the station with a train for Wadebridge and Padstow. The station was far bigger than the level of traffic warranted. In addition it was inconveniently situated on the northern edge of the town. The service was withdrawn in 1967.

Now : 31 March 1996

No trace remains of the station other than some railings from the fence that once adjoined the platform. The rest of the site is occupied by large retail shops, a supermarket and its car park. *Both Author*

326 LITTLE PETHERICK CREEK

Then : c1957

Little Petherick Creek joins the River Camel to the south of Padstow and was spanned by this steel bridge. 'T9' No 30715 has just crossed the structure with a train from Wadebridge, and with less than a mile to go, will soon reach the end of the line at Padstow.

Now : 31 March 1996

The bridge has now been incorporated into the Camel Trail. Although the railway has long gone, the bridge continues to provide an essential service for the thousands of people who walk or cycle across it every year. *Colin Hogg/Author*

327 PADSTOW

Then : undated but c1950

This is the end of our journey over the Southern, but it is only beginning for 'T9' No 30712, which is leaving the station with a typical local train of the 1950s. This picture gives an especially good view of the terminus, 259¾ miles from Waterloo. On the far left of the picture is the Metropole Hotel, then the station, with a long rake of coaches in the siding. To their right is the warehouse and fish market, and finally, the turntable from which a splendid view could be obtained down the estuary towards Padstow Bay. After having served local communities and visitors so well for almost 68 years, the line closed in January 1967.

Now : 31 March 1996

Growth of high bushes on the cliff which borders the landward side of station yard prevented me from reaching the exact position of the earlier picture. However, this view shows how little remains of the station infrastructure, apart from the fish market and the station house on the extreme left of the picture. Happily Padstow itself is still as attractive a resort as ever. *B. A. Butt/Author*

CALSTOCK

Then : 24 June 1961

At Calstock the line to Callington crossed the River Tamar into Cornwall, by means of a fine 12 arch, 129ft high viaduct. 'O2' No 30225 has just crossed the viaduct with this train for Callington, and is about to stop at the station which is located just behind the photographer.

Now : 1 April 1996

Services between Plymouth to Callington, the 'Tamar Valley Line' as it is now known, consist of some eight trains in each direction Monday to Saturday. This is the 11.30 train from Plymouth, which is due at Calstock at 12.02.

D.M. Hepburne-Scott (Rail Archive Stephenson)/Author